CHOMSKY
FOR BEGINNERS

DAVID COGSWELL

ILLUSTRATED BY PAUL GORDON

Writers and Readers Publishing, Inc.
P.O. Box 461, Village Station
New York, NY 10014

Writers and Readers Limited
9 Cynthia Street
London N1 9JF
England

A Writers and Readers Documentary Comic Book
Copyright © 1996
ISBN 0-86316-233-9
1 2 3 4 5 6 7 8 9 0

Manufactured in the United States of America

Beginners Documentary Comic Books are published by Writers and Readers Publishing, Inc. Its trademark, consisting of the words "For Beginners, Writers and Readers Documentary Comic Books" and the Writers and Readers logo, is registered in the U.S. Patent and Trademark Office and in other countries.

Contents

Noam Chomsky and the MEDIA: Can You Believe What You See and Hear? 69

Chomsky on POLITICS 103

Abbreviations of sources of quotes.

AC -- *After the Cataclysm*, Noam Chomsky and Edward S. Herman, 1979, South End Press.

APNM -- *American Power and the New Mandarins*, Noam Chomsky, 1967, 1969, Pantheon.

ATS -- *Aspects of The Theory of Syntax*, Noam Chomsky, 1965, MIT press.

CR -- *The Chomsky Reader*, ed. Richard Peck, 1987, Pantheon Books.

DD -- *Deterring Democracy*, Noam Chomsky, 1991, 1992, Hill and Wang.

ESP -- *Equality and Social Policy*, Noam Chomsky, 1978, University of Illinois Press.

FRS -- *For Reasons of State*, Noam Chomsky, 1970, 1971, 1972, Pantheon.

FT -- *The Fateful Triangle*, Noam Chomsky, 1983, South End Press.

INT -- Interview with Noam Chomsky, Sept. 14, 1993, David Cogswell

L&P -- *Language and Politics*, by Noam Chomsky, 1988, Black Rose Books.

MC -- *Manufacturing Consent*, Edward S. Herman and Noam Chomsky, 1988, Pantheon Books.

MCF -- *Manufacturing Consent: Noam Chomsky and the Media*. A film by Mark Achbar and Peter Wintonick in association with the Canadian Film...

NI -- *Necessary Illusions*, Noam Chomsky, 1989, South End Press.

NCZM -- Noam Chomsky writing in *Z Magazine*.

PE -- *Pirates and Emperors*, Noam Chomsky, 1986, Amana Books.

PD -- "The Panama Deception," a film by the Empowerment Project, 1992.

RC -- *Rethinking Camelot*, Noam Chomsky, 1993, South End Press.

TNCW -- *Towards a New Cold War, Essays on the current crisis and how we got there*, Noam Chomsky, 1982, Pantheon.

TT -- *Turning the Tide*, Noam Chomsky, 1985, South End Press.

WC -- *The Washington Connection and Third World Fascism*, Noam Chomsky and Edward S. Herman, 1979, South End Press.

WUS -- *What Uncle Sam Really Wants*, Noam Chomsky, 1986-92, Odonian Press.

Y5 -- *Year 501*, Noam Chomsky, 1993, South End Press.

Editor's note: Actual quotes by Chomsky are denoted with quotation marks and abbreviations indicating the source of the quote.

Introduction

Noam Chomsky is one of the ten most-quoted writers of all time.

The *Chicago Tribune* has called Professor Chomsky **"the most cited living author,"** adding that among intellectual luminaries of all eras, he ranks eighth, just behind Plato and Sigmund Freud.

6 — Plato

7 — Freud

8 — Chomsky

"To confront a mind that radically alters our perception of the world is one of life's most unsettling, yet liberating experiences,"

...writes James Peck in the Introduction to *The Chomsky Reader.* "In all American history, no one's writings are more unsettling than Noam Chomsky's.... No intellectual tradition quite captures his voice.... No party claims him; he is a spokesman for no ideology."

And the Mother of American newspapers, *The New York Times,* called Noam Chomsky **"arguably the most important intellectual alive."**

Noam Who?

In the 1990s, this is still the most frequent response to the mention of the name of **Noam Chomsky,** a mild-mannered professor of linguistics at the Massachusetts Institute of Technology.

(Why, you might wonder, have so many of us never heard of someone so "famous?" Is this the ultimate Yogi-Berra-ism—He's so famous no one's ever heard of him?)

The reason you haven't heard much about Noam Chomsky (which, by the way, is a demonstration in action of his thesis that the Media manipulates /distorts/withholds information to suit their owners) is because the gentlemen who own the Major Media don't want you to know about Noam Chomsky.

If too many people listen open-mindedly to what Chomsky has to say about huge corporations running the country, the world, both political parties, and the Major Media...why, the whole gingerbread fantasy we've been fed about America might vanish like the Emperor's clothes.

One of the wonderful things about Chomsky is that he makes us feel smart. Though our leaders have lied to us and played us for fools, and the Media has parroted their lies, even the most naive of us have known that we were not being given "the truth, the whole truth and nothing but the truth." We have even intuitively grasped the basic principles underlying many of Chomsky's views, even if we couldn't quite explain them. We may not understand the subtleties of the systems that control our lives, but many of us have noticed at least in part, several important truths:

Our government often lies to us.

Our government serves the needs of some and ignores the needs of others.

Our economic system is rigged.

With regard to most of the issues that affect most of the people, the major political parties are virtually identical.

The news media do not give a full, balanced picture of political events.

Though the United States is called a democracy, most of us are locked out of any meaningful participation in the decision-making process of our own country.

Above all, our government, our politicians, and our media, ignore the needs of the majority and serve the needs of the rich.

Things seem to be getting worse.

Note: These are not Chomsky's words, nor are they paraphrases — they are the author's interpretations.

Noam Chomsky has articulated a system of ideas that can help us make sense of our intuitions and misgivings—and to know which are justified and which are not. Because Chomsky's ideas about politics are antithetical to the purposes of the mass media—and to the rich gentlemen who own them—his ideas are rarely encountered in the mainstream. ("These institutions are not self-destructive, after all," he says.)

This documentary comic book is an attempt to help remedy that situation by presenting Chomsky's ideas to people who have not been exposed to them. It does not presume to sum up the work of Noam Chomsky. It is meant as a general introduction, an attempt to begin to answer the question "Who?" and an invitation to those who are unfamiliar with his ideas to look for themselves into the very pressing issues that he raises.

For those who may be completely unfamiliar with Noam Chomsky, let us begin by noting that Chomsky is known to the world for his work in two distinct areas. He first became famous through his work in linguistics, the study of language itself.

Chomsky's second career, as a political and social analyst and critic, is harder to categorize. It was his passion long before he became involved in linguistics, and it is what he has written most of his many books about. But if Chomsky had not first established such a distinguished reputation as a scientist, his radical political ideas would probably be even less heard of in the mainstream than they are.

Like Einstein's theory of Relativity, Chomsky's ideas about linguistics have spread in their influence, and their effects are gradually filtering down to the lives of ordinary people. But his work as a social and political theorist and as a "media critic" is of pressing importance right now to everyone who is concerned about the survival of democratic institutions, the protection of human rights and freedom, and the preservation of a habitable environment. It is this work that is of most pressing relevance to the general public. Chomsky is not a philosopher you leave in the classroom; he helps you live your life.

And don't worry—Chomsky is not a difficult read.

Chomsky is common sense elevated to genius.

Life is like a box of chocolates...

First, a little background: **How did Noam Chomsky come to be one of the ten most-quoted authors of all time, "arguably the most important intellectual alive."?**

Well, among other things, he was a college drop-out...

The File on Chomsky
A Biographical Sketch

SIGH...

Chomsky is reluctant to talk about his life. "I'm rather against the whole notion of making public personalities, of having some people be stars and all that," he says. Cults of personality distract people from real issues. The media are so absorbed with these public personalities, that "air time" is almost totally dominated with gossip, the details of hideous violent crimes, or sports. There is little information about anything you can do anything constructive about, including most of what your government is doing.

But though Chomsky may feel that the biographical details of his life are a distraction from the pressing issues that he wants to discuss, others are irresistibly curious about the lives of the originators of great ideas. Therefore we will take a quick look. But in deference to the man, we won't spend very long on the subject.

9

Abbe · Billy · Jenny · Noam

vram Noam Chomsky was born in Philadelphia, Pennsylvania, USA, on December 7, 1928. One of two sons, Chomsky was a child during the Great Depression, which began with the stock market crash in 1929 and lasted until World War II. The Chomsky family was spared the worst aspects of the Depression because both parents had jobs. The effects of the crisis were still profound, however, and Chomsky says that some of his earliest memories are Depression scenes: people selling rags at the door, police violently breaking strikes, and so on.

His parents both worked as Hebrew teachers. Noam's father William Chomsky was a noted Hebrew scholar and the author of *Hebrew, the Eternal Language*, one of the most popular books about the Hebrew language, published in 1958.

The family was deeply involved in Jewish culture, the Zionist movement, and the revival of the Hebrew language.

From age two to age 12, Chomsky attended an experimental progressive school where there were no grades, where there was no such thing as competition, and no such thing as a good student.

His family was practically the only Jewish family in a bitterly anti-Semitic Irish and German Catholic neighborhood where there was open support for the Nazis until the U.S. entered World War II. Chomsky was exposed to anti-Semitism on the streets and profoundly affected by the rise of fascism in Europe during the '30s.

His first published piece of writing was an editorial for his school newspaper about the fall of Barcelona. At the age of 12 he wrote a history of the Spanish Civil War.

"It was really a lament about the rise of fascism."

The Kiosk

He often visited an uncle in New York City who operated a magazine kiosk at the subway exit at 72nd and Broadway. Chomsky says his uncle was a hunchback with a background in "crime and left-wing politics." Because of his disability, he qualified to operate a kiosk. It was at the less trafficked exit of the subway entrance and did poorly as a business, but in the late '30s it became a hangout

for European emigres. Young Chomsky spent many hours there participating in lively discussions of issues and ideas that took place on an almost ongoing basis. Chomsky says the kiosk was where he received his political education. His uncle was also well-versed in the work of Sigmund Freud, and Chomsky developed a broad understanding of Freudian theory while still a teenager.

Dinner ready?...

In New York he was exposed to the Jewish working class intellectual culture with its concern for solidarity and socialist values. His aunts and uncles were materially poor but intellectually rich and maintained a tradition of lively discussion and penetrating inquiry into social and political processes.

In New York he discovered the anarchist book shops on Fourth Avenue where he would often browse and read.

Chomsky has described an experience that affected him deeply in which a bully was picking on "the standard fat kid," and everyone supported the bully while no one came to the aid of the victim.

"I stood up for him for a while," he says. "Then I got scared." Afterwards he was ashamed and resolved that in the future he would support the underdog, those unjustly oppressed. "I was always on the side of the losers," he said, "like the Spanish anarchists."

13

Though Chomsky is known for his intellect, his political ideas are driven more by moral principles. He was appalled by the way people taunted German prisoners through the barbed wire at a prison camp near his high school as though it was the patriotic thing to do to. At the same time, Chomsky was much more passionately opposed to Nazism than the people who were taunting the soldiers.

On the day of the Hiroshima bombing, says Chomsky, "I literally couldn't talk to any one. There was nobody. I just walked off by myself... I could never talk to anyone about it and never understood anyone's reaction."
[CR]

That's a pretty big cloud hanging over your head...

College Dropout

To manage the expense of college, he commuted several hours a day to attend the university while living at home. He also worked as a Hebrew teacher evenings, afternoons, and Sundays. But his enthusiasm for the university waned. He lost interest in every subject he enrolled in. After two years, he decided to drop out. But he maintained his lifelong

interest in radical politics and became even more deeply involved in Zionism activities. Many years later, in upholding many of the same principles, he would be called anti-Zionist.

O-K, forget it... let's turn this thing around...

Chomsky considered going to Palestine to help to further Arab-Jewish cooperation within a socialist framework. But he was put off by the "deeply anti-democratic" concept of a Jewish state.

Through his political interests Chomsky met **Zellig Harris**, a teacher of linguistics at the University of Pennsylvania. Chomsky was one of many who found Harris immensely appealing. Harris shared many of Chomsky's political passions, so he enrolled in Harris' graduate classes. The first reading he did in the field of linguistics was of proofs of Harris' Methods of Structural Linguistics, which was published several years later.

At Harris' suggestion, Chomsky began taking courses in philosophy and mathematics. He had no background in them, but found them fascinating.

Under Harris' influence, Chomsky returned to college and studied linguistics. He calls his university experience "unconventional." The linguistics department was a small group of graduate students who shared political and other interests and met in restaurants or in Harris' apartment for all-day discussion sessions. Chomsky immersed himself in linguistics, philosophy, and logic. He was awarded BA and MA degrees though he had very little contact with the university system. He married linguist Carol Schaz in 1949. They were to have a son and two daughters.

One of Chomsky's philosophy teachers was Nelson Goodman, who introduced him to the Society of Fellows at Harvard. He was admitted in 1951 and awarded a stipend, which freed him for the first time in his life from the necessity to work outside of his research.

In 1953, while a member of the Society of Fellows, Chomsky went to Israel and lived on a kibbutz for a few months. There was little food and the work was hard, but Chomsky enjoyed it. He saw the kibbutz as a functioning and successful libertarian community.

Chomsky and his wife considered going back to live on the kibbutz. He had no hopes or interest in an academic career and nothing holding him in the United States. But he was uncomfortable with the conformism and the racist principles underlying the institution. Chomsky had been opposed to the formation of a Jewish state in 1947-48 because he felt the socialist institutions of the pre-state Jewish settlement in Palestine would not survive the state system.

When his term at Society of Fellows was scheduled to end in 1954 he had no job prospects, so he asked for an extension. His wife had gone back to the kibbutz for a longer visit and the two planned to return to stay. Instead Chomsky received a research position at M.I.T. and became immersed in linguistics.

In 1955 he received a Ph.D. from the University of Pennsylvania on the basis of his submission of a chapter of a book he was working on. Though the book was virtually complete in 1956, it was so unconventional at the time that it was not published until 1975, and then only in part, as *Logical Structure of Linguistic Theory.*

Well, it's an interesting book, Mr. Chomsky, albeit a little unconventional. Perhaps we'll publish part of it sometime soon...

Political activism

In the 1960's the escalation of the Vietnam war forced Chomsky to make a moral choice. He began active resistance to the war knowing that it was very likely that he would have to spend time in prison for it. He put a very comfortable position in academia in jeopardy to protest the war. Asked about why he took that risk, Chomsky has said, **"It has to do with being able to look yourself in the eye in the morning."**

In 1966, Chomsky wrote an article called "The Responsibility of Intellectuals" which appeared in *The New York Review of Books*. The article was widely acclaimed around the world. In publishing the article, Chomsky was acting on the responsibility that the article referred to:

"Intellectuals are in a position to expose the lies of governments, to analyze actions according to their causes and motives and often hidden intentions. In the Western world at least, they have the power that comes from political liberty, from access to information and freedom of expression. For a privileged minority, Western democracy provides the leisure, the facilities and the training to seek the truth lying hidden behind the veil of distortion and misrepresentation, ideology, and class interest through which the events of current history are presented to us...

"American aggressiveness, however it may be masked in pious rhetoric, is a dominant force in world affairs and must be analyzed in terms of its causes and motives."

[*NY Review of Books.]

Not long after that article appeared, the *New York Review of Books* stopped publishing submissions by Chomsky. America's top intellectuals didn't take kindly to being told that they were little more than flunkies who dressed the lies of the ruling class in fancy language and looked the other way when their own government committed atrocities that they wouldn't hesitate to condemn if they'd been perpetrated by any other country. To the ruthlessly honest Chomsky, you judged your friends, your enemies, and yourself by the same set of rules.

Anything else would be cheating, wouldn't it?

In October 1967, Chomsky participated in the demonstrations that took place at the Pentagon and the Justice Department and was one of many who were jailed. Norman Mailer, who shared a cell with Chomsky described him in

The Armies of the Night, as "a slim, sharp-featured man with an ascetic expression and an air of gentle but absolute moral integrity."

Since making the commitment to be politically active in the late '60s, P r o f e s s o r Chomsky has written a steady stream of books, articles, and p a m p h l e t s expressing his views. He appears almost anywhere he is invited to speak or discuss his views. In the meantime, he remains a professor of linguistics at MIT.

Despite the variety of his interests and pursuits, Chomsky's approach is amazingly consistent. **He applies the same ruthlessly honest logic to everything he examines.** He did not, however, spring forth fully formed, fully "Chomskian."

As with any important thinker, Chomsky's system of ideas rests on the work of many fine thinkers who preceded him.

We'll have a look at some of the more notable ones.

The Shoulders of Giants —
Antecedents to the Thinking of Chomsky

Plato (428-354 B.C.)

Chomsky, along with every thinker in the tradition of Western Philosophy, owes something to Plato for laying a foundation for philosophy with his dedication to truth-seeking and his concern for developing a rational moral personality.

Plato asked, ***"How can a human know so much that he seems to have had little evidence for?"*** Chomsky asks the same question about the way children easily master language.

In Chomsky's approach to the study of linguistics and the cognitive processes, he, like Plato, searches for abstract and ideal forms as explanations rather than merely drawing generalizations from observations.

In Plato's *Republic*, he envisioned an ideal society in which justice is the ruling principle, an ideal which Chomsky would share. But Chomsky deviates from

Plato's belief in the establishment of a heirarchy which places intellectuals in a privileged class.

Plato rejected democracy because in it political power is not attached to special qualifications. Chomsky prizes the democratic principle. Both reject tyranny, the exercise of irresponsible power by amoral men of criminal will.

Rene Descartes (1596-1650)

Descartes is often called "The Father of Modern Philosophy."

Chomsky says that he believes in "Cartesian common sense," the scientific method as laid out in *Discourse on Method* by Descartes. In it, Descartes lays out rules to help navigate safely through chains of logic to reach reliable, though limited conclusions.

Descartes began by rejecting all philosophy before him and attempting to establish reliable premises upon which to build a system of thought that would yield the truth.

He had a dream that convinced him that, since the senses may deceive us, all true knowledge must come from reason alone.

He had so much trouble finding any premises that he could believe in that he finally broke everything down to one basic principle. All he could be sure of, he said, was that he was thinking. From that he reasoned that it was safe to say he must exist. **"I think therefore I am"** became the starting premise of his philosophy.

His method for thinking logically toward reliable conclusions included the following rules:

• **Accept only clear and distinct ideas.**
• **Break each problem into as many parts as necessary to solve it.**
• **Work from the simple to the complex.**
• **Always check for mistakes.**

In all of Chomsky's thinking, he adheres tightly to these basic principles. In linguistics he moves beyond mere observation and tries to establish explanatory principles. He also brings scientific discipline to his observations of politics and the functioning of media.

Descartes tried to discover the principles that determined how we learn by looking at the difference between data (input) and knowledge (represented by output).

When I see an irregular figure, why do I see it as a triangle? Why do I interpret the input of an imperfect or degenerate triangle as an ideal shape in my mind?

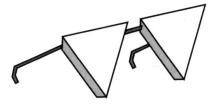

Descartes observed the discrepancy between the figure we are presented and the triangle we construct in our minds and argued that we see a triangle because there is something about the nature of our minds that makes the image of a triangle easily constructible by the mind, a kind of schema or template that we impose over the data of perception.

Chomsky asks...

Why do children learn a specific system of grammar over all the other ones that might possibly be constructed from the input of the child's experience?

Chomsky follows the Cartesian example in his method of studying linguistics. He uses his observations as a **jumping off point** for abstract thinking and attempts to establish abstract principles.

And now...
a swan dive for
science...

In *Meditations on the First Philosophy: Of Truth and Error,* Descartes says,

"I am conscious that I possess a certain faculty of judging [or distinguishing truth from error], which I doubtless received from God, along with whatever else is mine; and since it is impossible that he should will to deceive me, it is likewise certain that he has not given me a faculty that will ever lead me into error, provided I use it aright."

For Descartes man's nature is unique in quality and comes from God.

Chomsky puts this idea in a modern scientific context by speculating that sudden and dramatic mutations may have led to qualities of intelligence that are, as far as we know, unique to humans.

Language is the most universal and characteristic of these qualities, though Chomsky allows that the same kind of uniqueness may be found in other areas as well. The study of language may offer a wedge, he says, or a model through which to gain a broader understanding of qualities that are uniquely human.

Jean Jacques Rousseau (1712 - 1778)

In *Discourse on Equality*, Rousseau challenged the legitimacy of nearly every social institution. This was a central theme of the US Declaration of Independence and the Constitution, to challenge the legitimacy of every institution, and to keep on challenging it (as Chomsky has) with "eternal vigilance."

The American system was designed with a view of human institutions that was not innocent. Power corrupts, so watch it. Freedom should never be taken for granted.

Rousseau also condemned the individual control of property and wealth. He called them "usurpations by the rich... established only by force, and force could take them away without [the rich] having grounds for complaint."

It violates natural law that a handful of men be glutted with superfluities while the starving multitude lacks necessities.

Chomsky's sense of social justice owes a great deal to Rousseau—he cannot imagine why a society filled with free people tolerate "a handful of men" to be "glutted with superfluities while the starving multitude lacks necessities."

Rousseau said the establishment of civil society is a conspiracy by the rich to guarantee their plunder. The rich "institute regulations of justice and peace to which all are obliged to conform." (As Anatole France would later say, these laws deny to the rich and the poor equally the right to sleep under the bridge at night.)

The poor and weak were seduced by such laws, said Rousseau. "All ran to meet their chains thinking they secured their freedom..."

It is not so much understanding which constitutes the distinction of man among the animals, as it is his being a free agent.

For Rousseau, the essence of human nature is human freedom and the consciousness of this freedom. To Rousseau, surrendering your freedom was an insult to God.

Chomsky's political stand is often classified as "leftist" or "socialist" or "anarchist" and as such he is foolishly dismissed by many who have come to associate those words with the darkest evil. But the principles that he champions most are freedom and democracy.

In the most basic sense, democracy means rule by the people, the majority. It is a principle that may be applied to a system, it is not a system itself. There are many different ways to apply democratic principles to public policy. In the United States, the democratic principle is applied through people having the right to vote for office-holders who make the decisions. Theoretically all citizens have equal voting rights. In practice, it is not the voters who make government policy, but the elected officials.

In America, the control of the country's resources and wealth are most definitely not distributed democratically. On the contrary, America's wealth and resources are very undemocratically concentrated in the hands of a tiny minority.

Wilhelm von Humboldt (1767 – 1835)

Chomsky found in Humboldt an affinity in both political ideas and linguistic ideas. He credits Humboldt with having a concept similar to Chomsky's generative grammar. But Humboldt lacked the mathematical techniques for developing it. Chomsky studied the foundations of mathematics without thinking it had any relationship to linguistics.

He soon discovered that he could apply his mathematical insights to generative grammar.

Chomsky called Humboldt...

Who do you think you are... Wilhelm von Humboldt?

1 + 1 = cat

"One of the most profound theorists of general linguistics and an early and forceful advocate of libertarian values." [CR].

John Stuart Mill's essay "On Liberty" began with a quote of the "leading principle" of Humboldt's thought: **"the absolute and essential importance of human development in its richest diversity."** Humboldt concludes his critique of the authoritarian state by saying: **"I have felt myself animated throughout with a sense of the deepest respect for the inherent dignity of human nature, and for freedom, which alone befits that dignity."**(FRS)

Humboldt believed that nothing better prepares people for freedom than freedom itself. By loosening the bonds on all people, he said, "We shall progress at every step." Like Rousseau he believed that humans are creative and searching beings. "To inquire and to create -- these are the centers around which all human pursuits more or less directly revolve." And the freedom to express this humanness should not only be for the elite, but for everyone. "There is something degrading to human nature in the idea of refusing to any man the right to be a man."

Karl Marx
(1818-1883)

"LONDON --
September 18, 1861.
Mrs. Beecher Stowe's letter to Lord Shaftesbury, whatever its intrinsic merit may be, has done a great deal of good by forcing the anti-Northern organs of the London press to speak out and lay before the general public the ostensible reasons for their hostile tone against the North and their ill-concealed sympathies with the South, which looks rather strange on the part of people affecting an utter horror of slavery. Their first main grievance is that the present American war is `not one for the abolition of slavery,' and that, therefore, the high-minded Britisher, used to undertake wars of his own and interest himself in other people's wars only on the basis of `broad humanitarian principles,' cannot be expected to feel any sympathy with his Northern cousins.

'In the first place,' says *The Economist*, 'the assumption that the quarrel between the North and South is a quarrel between Negro freedom on the one side and Negro slavery on the other is as impudent as it is untrue.' 'The North,' says *The Saturday Review*, 'does not proclaim Abolition, and never pretended to fight for anti-slavery. The North has not hoisted for its oriflamme the sacred symbol of justice to the Negro; its cri de guerre is not unconditional abolition.' 'If,' says *The Examiner*, 'we have been deceived about the real significance of the sublime movement, who but the Federalists themselves have to answer for the deception?' "

—Karl Marx, writing in the *New York Daily Tribune* and the *Vienna Presse*

This is remarkably similar to Chomsky's critiques of what he reads in newspapers. In fact Chomsky acknowledges a debt to Marx. Chomsky's uncles and aunts in New York were part of the Jewish radical intelligentsia who dealt daily in discourse about class struggle.

Many members of that community were members of the Communist Party in its earlier days, but Chomsky says he grew out of that phase when he was 12 or 13. Many of the early communists later became members of an anti-Bolshevik left that looked upon the Russian revolution as a right-wing perversion of Marxism.

What Chomsky gained from Marx was the idea that societies are made up of economic classes and that analyzing them on that basis helps to understand social processes. But Chomsky did not agree with the conclusions Marx drew from his analysis and questioned whether they were even applicable a century later.

He was repelled by Marx's idea of a "dictatorship of the proletariat," being himself a lover of democracy. For the same reason he found the Soviet system abhorrent, but questioned whether it really had much to do with Marx. Soviet communism took its character from its leader Vladimir Lenin. Lenin's actions once he took power in Russia are very much in contradiction with his writings.

"There's a big difference between the libertarian doctrines of a person who is trying to associate himself with a mass popular movement to acquire power and the authoritarian power of somebody who's taken power and is trying to consolidate it," [L&P]

George Orwell
(1903-1950)

In the preface to *Knowledge of Language* Chomsky asks how people can know so little about the structure and function of their society, given so much evidence. He calls it "Orwell's problem," and defines it

as "the ability of totalitarian systems to instill beliefs that are firmly held and widely accepted although they are completely without foundation and often plainly at variance with obvious facts about the world around us."

George Orwell was the pen name of Eric Arthur Blair, who was born in 1903 in Motihari, India, the son of an English colonial minister. Orwell created a framework for the analysis of political propaganda and thought control that has become part of modern folklore.

Unfortunately, the users of propaganda have probably learned more from Orwell's analyses than those who are the target of brainwashing.

Orwell's book *Homage to Catalonia* (1938) came out of his own experiences when he joined the Loyalists in Spain and was severely wounded during the Spanish Civil War. Orwell saw the pioneering days of Fascism in its testing grounds in Spain under the dictator Franco. The characteristics of fascism which were to become familiar include: concentrated private control of resources and wealth, control of

I **must** write about this some day...

information, massive investment in the manufacture of arms and military equipment; suppression of labor movements and popular democratic movements; military actions to expand territory, and so on.

Fascism was a natural outgrowth of monarchy. It was an industrial-age descendant of aristocracy that developed when it was discovered that war production could generate tremendous wealth.

Casualties?

Profits!

THE WAR

Orwell's novel, 1984 (published in 1949), portrayed a world in which three major superpowers maintained constant war, shifting enemies periodically. War was essential to the state, to the operation of its economy and its control structures.

Many of the concepts and expressions from 1984 (e.g., Thoughtcrime and the Thought Police) have become familiar parts of our language. The Ministry of Truth was the place where, Winston, the hero of 1984 worked, "cleansing" news reports and altering the public record day to day as it served the purposes of the leaders. Newspeak is the name for the language that the government used to hide what it was doing. Using techniques such as oversimplification, euphemism, misrepresentation, abbreviation, blurring and reversal of meaning, Newspeak makes language so meaningless that it cannot be used to communicate—or even to understand—the activities of the state.

"Don't you see that the whole aim of Newspeak is to narrow the range of thought? In the end we shall make thought-crime literally impossible, because there will be no words in which to express it.... Every year...the range of consciousness [grows]... a little smaller..."

From **1984**, George Orwell.

Doublethink and doublespeak refer to the use of words to mean their opposite, a tactic used by governments to obscure the real meaning of what they are doing. "Pacification" will be used to describe an invasion, for example. Remember "tax simplification?"

Got that new simplified tax form right here...

Orwell's 1946 essay "Politics and the English Language" is an excellent analysis of how the corruption of language is related to political control. In it he describes how language can be used to manipulate, to mislead.

"In our time, political speech and writing are largely the defense of the indefensible," he says, sounding remarkably like Chomsky would

later. **"Defenseless villages are bombarded from the air, the inhabitants driven out into the countryside, the cattle machine-gunned, the huts set on fire with incendiary bullets: this is called pacification. Millions of peasants are robbed of their farms and sent trudging along the roads with no more than they can carry: this is called transfer of population or rectification of frontiers.**

People are imprisoned for years without trial, or shot in the back of the neck or sent to die of scurvy in Arctic lumber camps: this is called elimination of unreliable elements. Such phraseology is needed if one wants to name something without calling up mental pictures of it. Consider for instance some comfortable English professor defending Russian totalitarianism. He cannot say outright, 'I believe in killing

off your opponents when you can get good results by doing so.' Probably, therefore, he will say something like this:

'While freely conceding that the Soviet regime exhibits certain features which the humanitarian may be inclined to deplore, we must, I think, agree that a certain curtailment of the right to political opposition is an unavoidable concomitant of transitional periods, and that the rigors which the Russian people have been called upon to undergo have been amply justified in the sphere of concrete achievement.'

"When there is a gap between one's real and one's declared aims, one turns...instinctively to long words...like a cuttlefish squirting out ink."

The anarchist tradition

Anarchism is commonly defined as the belief in the abolishment of all forms of organized government, laws and machinery of law enforcement. In Chomsky's view, it is not the lack of organized government, but a different shape of organization that is not hierarchical. It's based on finding forms of social organization that are viable alternatives to centralized state power and coercive institutions.

At one point Chomsky defines the anarchist vision as seeking "a community of free-association without coercion by the state or other authoritarian institutions in which free men can create and inquire and achieve the highest development of their powers."

In real life, there are no pure representations of any theory of social or economic organization, only societies in which different theories and philosophies are applied to the real circumstances of life.

Zellig Harris

When Chomsky met Zellig Harris, he was on the verge of dropping out of college, having found that every course he took soured his previous interest in the subject. Politics was always his passion and Harris shared many of his political inclinations. It was largely this shared interest that led Chomsky into linguistics, though language was also a major interest of Chomsky's going back to his childhood when his parents were language teachers.

Harris did a series of studies that led to the development of techniques for the scientific study of meaning, and to a revolution in linguistics. He extended structuralist analysis beyond the sentence and developed formulas to capture systematic linguistic relationships between different kinds of sentences. He called his formulas transformations. Chomsky incorporated the concept of transformation into what he called transformative-generative linguistics, or simply generative linguistics.

A Note to the Reader:

For those of you who can't wait to sink your teeth into Chomsky's "juicy" work on Politics and Media, by all means feel free to skip ahead to the sections dealing with those exciting subjects. But if you do choose to read the other sections first, please come back and read the section on Linguistics.

Before Chomsky came out as a harsh critic of American foreign policy—and of *The New York Times* itself—even The Times enthusiastically acknowledged his importance as a pioneer in linguistics, saying that his first book *Syntactic Structures*, had created **"The Chomskyan Revolution in Linguistics."** He was routinely referred to in newsmedia ShortThink as **"The Einstein of Linguistics."**

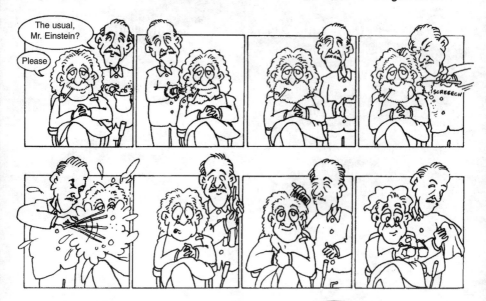

But even more importantly, Chomsky's evolution into the most penetrating social critic of our time developed logically, and in a sense morally, out of his work on linguistics. If at times, his social criticism is so harsh that one is tempted to wonder if Chomsky has a low view of humanity, his work in linguistics reveals a view of human nature that is so positive and hopeful that it's almost religious. Do yourself a favor and check it out.

44

Linguistics

What is linguistics?

Linguistics is the science of language. In using language, people employ principles of grammar, the complex and subtle rules of language use, without having to consciously know the principles. Part of the work of linguistics is to discover or establish those principles.

Another part of the work of linguistics is to compare and contrast languages, their grammars, pronunciations, how meaning is created and how the languages are used. As with other studies, early biology for example, a preliminary part of the task is naming and classification.

Modern linguistics emerged as a distinct field of study in the 19th Century while colonialism was flourishing, world travel was increasing, and European cultures were encountering other cultures and languages. Linguists made an effort to study the languages that they were encountering, in many cases languages that were disappearing under the pressure of colonialism. Experts in linguistics have often been called upon to ease confrontations between cultures by helping people to learn foreign languages as quickly as possible.

But we're getting ahead of ourselves.

Evolution of linguistics

In the West, the study of language began with the Greeks. For Plato it was a study of the etymologies or origins of Greek words. **Dionysius Thrax**, in the 1st Century BC., worked out an elaborate system of grammar for the Greek language. It became known as **traditional grammar**.

Roman grammarians Aelius Donatus and Priscian in the 6th Century AD. adopted Dionysius Thrax's system and adapted it to Latin. It worked well because the two languages are both Indo-European languages, related in lineage and structurally similar.

The Greeks philosophical grammar was passed onto the Romans. The Graeco-Roman tradition extended into Medieval times when it was applied to the modern European languages. When Latin branched into the Romance languages—Italian, French, and Spanish— the languages had become structurally different and required different kinds of analysis. It became difficult to apply the traditional grammar.

Some scholars saw the changes as a corruption of classical Latin and urged return to the archaic language forms. The idea that language change is corruption and should be prevented is called linguistic prescriptivism.

46

With the 15th century exploration of trade routes and colonization, Europe was exposed to other languages not descended from Latin or Greek and not subject to the same traditional grammar. This stimulated a search for principles that would apply to the broadened frame of reference of languages.

The search for canons of a universal logic led to the so-called general grammars of the 17th Century.

With the discovery of the New World, grammatical analysis was extended to non–European languages, but was relatively unproductive because all the languages were forced into the Latin mold. It was when the English discovered the methods of the Indian scholar Panini (c. 4th century B.C.) that modern linguistics began. Panini provided a new view of language and grammatical description.

The English colonists in India in the 18th Century discovered **Sanskrit**, an ancient language of religion, philosophy, and literature (now classified as an Indo-Iranian language). The Hindus held Sanskrit in esteem the way Europeans did Latin. Linguists saw a resemblance between Sanskrit and Greek and Latin.

SANSKRIT

English	Mother	is
Sanskrit	Mata	sti
Greek	Meter	esti
Latin	Mater	est

Specific words are similar, as are the organization of morphology and syntax.

morphology: form and structure of language

syntax: the way words are put together to form phrases, clauses, sentences...

Hindus had studied the grammar of Sanskrit for three millennia and their work in many respects went beyond the traditional grammar of the west in terms of philosophical consistency and analytic thoroughness. The sacred texts of India, the Vedas, were studied grammatically by tradition and the tradition was compiled by Panini, the precursor of modern linguistics.

Book report
by Panini

"Moby Dick"

$3 \times 48 = 144$

$3\sqrt{x} \div \frac{y}{2} = x^3$

$2 + 2 + 4 + 3 = 11$

$376^5 \sqrt{\pi^4 832}$

$.0567 \angle 4x^3$

He based his statements on the direct observation of the actual texts he analyzed, and he expressed them in quasi mathematical symbols. Panini's Sanskrit grammar became the model for European linguists. **In many aspects his methods have not been improved upon since.**

European scholars sought an explanation for the similarity of Sanskrit to Latin and Greek. **Sir William Jones**, considered the first great European scholar of Sanskrit, suggested in 1786 that the three languages may all "have sprung from some common source which, perhaps, no longer exists."

Jones' insight defined the area of study for linguists of the next 100 years. Nineteenth Century linguistics was primarily historical and comparative, as scholars looked for cross-connections and evolutionary links between Sanskrit, Greek, Latin, Germanic, Celtic and other Indo-European languages.

Toward the end of the 19th Century, linguists began to turn their attention from the history and evolution of language to its organization and function. This branch of study became known as synchronic linguistics, the study of the language now, as opposed to historical or diachronic linguistics. It was exemplified in the work of Swiss linguist **Ferdinand de Saussure** in his *Course in General Linguistics*, published posthumously in 1916. The two analytic modes remain today as complementary aspects of the study of linguistics.

During the 1920s synchronic linguistics in America was stimulated by study of a rich variety of **Native American languages**. Major linguists of the time, such as Franz Boas, Edward Sapir, and Alfred L. Kroeber, were also social anthropologists. In the early 1930s, linguists turned from descriptive work to a search for theoretical foundations. **Leonard Bloomfield**, a Behaviorist, laid down tenets of American linguistic thought in 1933 in his book *Language*.

Bloomfield's behaviorist model was refined in the generation that followed by such linguists as Bernard Bloch, Zellig Harris, Charles Hockett, Eugene Nida, and Kenneth Pike, who developed a theory of language analysis known as neo-Bloomfieldian or structural linguistics, called American structuralism to distinguish it from other branches called structural.

Behaviorism limited its field of inquiry to physically measurable phenomena, in an effort to emulate the physical sciences. Meaning, therefore, was not a part of the domain of the structuralists. In the early 1950s, however, Zellig Harris of the University of Pennsylvania began a series of studies that led to the development of techniques for the scientific study of meaning, and to a revolution in linguistics. He extended structuralist analysis beyond the sentence and developed formulas to capture systematic linguistic relationships between different kinds of sentences. He called his formulas transformations.

I was a student of Harris. I incorporated the concept of transformation into a theory now called TRANSFORMATIVE-GENERATIVE LINGUISTICS, *or simply* GENERATIVE LINGUISTICS. *The theory breaks off from structuralism in that it synthesizes theoretical and methodological elements from mathematics and the philosophy of language. I rebelled against behaviorism, taking a neo-rationalist stance which recalls the 17th Century concept of general grammar.*

The concept of transformations gave linguistics a powerful descriptive and analytic tool, and dropping the narrow limitations of Behaviorist doctrine opened a broad area for inquiry. Between 1960 and 1980, generative linguistics ascended and structuralism declined.

Linguistics as a science

Traditionally linguists studied the differences and similarities of languages in their pronunciation, grammar, vocabulary, and relationships between speakers. They created a vocabulary for the study of language which could be used by people in other fields who have an interest in language, such as lexicographers, speech therapists, translators and language teachers. Chomsky wanted linguistics to be "a real science."

In his own work, he adheres closely to the discipline of the scientific method. It has been a goal of Chomsky to move the study of linguistics beyond the "butterfly collecting" stage to a search for explanatory principles and beyond that, to being a key to the understanding of human nature. In this way linguistics moves from a pedestrian study that services other fields, to something powerful, with profound and far-reaching effects, like physics.

It has long been a disputed point whether or not the social sciences, studies of people, can really be called sciences. B.F. Skinner tried to apply a scientific point of view to the study of psychology, but by Chomsky's evaluation he failed because **he attempted to deal with human beings as though they were equivalent to inanimate objects.**

Chomsky's way of bringing science into humanistic studies would be not to view humans as equivalent to the objects of study of the physical sciences, but to adopt scientific methods of analysis and logic.

In his search for explanatory principles, Chomsky focused more on similarities between languages than on differences. He also narrowed his focus to English and well-studied languages rather than branching out and cataloging many obscure languages. Chomsky felt that science must make an attempt to explain why things function the way they do. Though many reject the idea that human behavior can be the subject of a scientific study, for Chomsky seeking solutions to problems, trying to find answers to the question **"why?"** is what characterizes science.

Chomsky used the science of physics as a model for how he envisioned linguistics. The relevant characteristics are:

1. It is important to seek explanations and not just descriptions and classifications.

2. Narrowing the field of study can lead to more firmly established theories though at a sacrifice to more far-reaching answers.

3. The use of abstraction and idealization constructs models that can be accorded a greater degree of reality than sensory data.

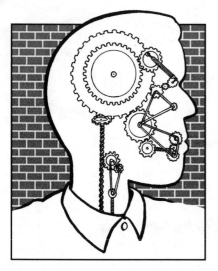

According to Chomsky, the central nervous system and cortex are biologically programmed not only for the physiological aspects of speech but also for the organization of language itself. The capacity for organizing words into relationships of words to each other is inherent.

The ordinary use of language, says Chomsky, is creative, innovative, and more than merely a response to a stimulus, as the Behaviorist model suggests. [see Behaviorism]

Universal Generative Grammar

Chomsky determined that there is a universal grammar which is part of the genetic birthright of human beings, that we are born with a basic template for language that any specific language fits into. This unique capacity for language is, as far as we know, unique to the human species and ordinary use of language is evidence of tremendous creative potential in every human being.

LANGUAGE

The remarkable ability of human children to rapidly learn language in their infancy when they still have little outside experience or frame of reference upon which to base their understanding, leads Chomsky to believe that not only the capacity for language, but a fundamental grammar is innate from birth.

It is relatively certain, says Chomsky, that people are not genetically programmed for a specific language, so that a Chinese baby growing up in the United States will speak English and an American child surrounded by people speaking Chinese will learn to speak Chinese. From this fact, says Chomsky, it follows by logic that there is a universal grammar which underlies the structure of all languages. Chomsky went on to formulate rules for this grammar. Employing a system of symbols, these formulations became increasingly like mathematical operations.

Evidence that Universal Grammar Is Innate

Chomsky says that certain rules of grammar are too hidden, too complex to be figured out by children who have so little evidence to go on. These skills are innate, he says, because they cannot have been learned. Children do not have enough evidence to piece together so complicated a system as grammar, to quickly learn to improvise sure-footedly within the system of grammar while rarely being told what the underlying rules are and rarely being given examples of incorrect grammar.

55

Language acquisition is distinguished by linguists from language learning. Learning a language later in life, after the developmental stage of language acquisition has played out, is much like other kinds of learning. Language students get books of grammar and vocabulary, take classes, are instructed and drilled by teachers. Young children who have never spoken before absorb language with great rapidity and with the minimum of cues from the outside world. The process of acquisition is akin to imprinting, an innate process which begins to play out along certain lines when it is triggered by outside stimuli.

When a bird hatches from its shell at birth and forms a parent/young bond with the first large organism it sees, it is called imprinting. It is a behavior that is triggered by some outside stimulus, but plays itself out in a standard, predictable way, and is the same from one individual to the next.

The question of nature versus nurture, of what is inherited genetically versus what is acquired through experience and environmental influences, is an old one. These categories cannot be clearly separated. They seem to blend together as they play out in the real world. So the controversy will probably never be clearly resolved. The behaviorist doctrine says that all behavior is learned and that human beings are a blank slate at birth and can be manipulated and molded to acquire almost any sort of behavior.

To Chomsky, this would be almost criminally simplistic and inconsistent with the facts. Language is exceedingly complex and yet is mastered easily in a very short time by human children who begin with no frame of reference at all and rarely receive any degree of formal instruction. The only evidence they have to work with is hearing people talk. They are rarely told why the sentences are correct or given examples of what would be incorrect. And yet they launch into the fluent

usage of a system that includes a large number of very complex principles of grammar, principles Chomsky says they have not received enough evidence to learn about. Chomsky establishes that it would not be possible for these principles to be learned with the evidence that is available to the child.

Two points that you surely noticed, but just in case you didn't:

1. Chomsky's view of humanity is startlingly positive: "[the] ordinary use of language is evidence of tremendous creative potential in every human being."

2. Chomsky's special genius in both linguistics and politics is his ability to see the clear, simple truth of things. Chomsky is the guy who notices that the Emperor isn't wearing any clothes. That's why he appeals to so many of us.

Some people would have been content to stop there—with the convincing argument that grammar was innate, not learned. Not Chomsky. He wanted the details. How can we prove that grammar is not learned? What does it mean to say that grammar is innate? What is grammar and how exactly does it work?

Is Grammar Learnable?

By analyzing subtle grammatical rules that are far beyond the awareness of the average speaker of English, Chomsky shows that the rules we are fluent in are too difficult to have figured out with the evidence we are given as children first learning to speak. Even trying to understand an explanation of how anaphors* (A linguist's term for a commonly-used but difficult-to-explain "binding" grammatical structure) work is difficult, and yet rarely is the mistake made in the language usage of ordinary people.

*__Editor's note__: *As if to prove Chomsky's point, the explanation of anaphors was so difficult, that out of mercy for the lay reader, we've decided to leave it out.*

It is difficult for a professional linguist to merely list, after the fact, all of the grammatical subtleties that go into making an acceptable or well-formed sentence, especially since the number of possible combinations seems limitless—some sentences are ambiguous, some are not; some are connected to others by paraphrases, implicational relations and so forth. Studying a simple paragraph yields a rich system of inter-relationships and cross-connections that are all consistent with a very subtle system of grammar.

Most sentences that are mathematically possible are clearly ungrammatical, and yet to pinpoint the reason for the unacceptability of a certain form, in many cases, is extremely difficult.

I repeat: Is grammar learnable?

The Study of Learning

To study learning, says Chomsky, we must look at the input (data) and output (grammar) in the organism (child). A child who has no knowledge of language to start with constructs a working knowledge of a language based on certain data. From the relationship of the input/data to the output/grammar, we may begin to develop some idea of the mental activities of the organism, the transition from input to output.

In order to account for the kinds of grammatical rules used in simple sentences, we have to postulate abstract structures that have no direct connection with the physical facts (data) and can only be reasoned from those facts by long chains of highly abstract mental operations.

How *do* we know that we can say (for example), "What box did Margaret keep the necklace in?" but not "What box did Margaret keep the necklace that was in?" It is a property of English, and probably all languages, that some complex noun phrases, like "the necklace that was in the box," cannot be kept intact when you change a statement to a question. Chomsky says this is a linguistic universal, but is unlearnable from the evidence. When we are learning the language, we are not given enough evidence from which to draw this conclusion.

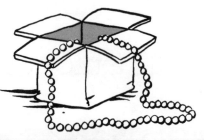

If we analyze these processes carefully, says Chomsky, we find that the picture does not fit the stimulus-response model of how learning takes place, the blank-slate model of the human organism as portrayed by the Behaviorists. The stimulus-response theory can only lead to a system of habits, a network of associations. And such a system will not account for the sound-meaning relation that all of us know intuitively when we have mastered our language.

The grammars that we use are creative in that they generate, specify, or characterize, a virtually infinite number of sentences. A speaker is capable of using and understanding sentences that have no physical similarity — no point-by-point relationship — to any sentence he has ever heard.

The Infinite Variety of Language

An interesting experiment in this regard was conducted by Richard Ohmann, a professor at Wesleyan University. He showed 25 people a simple cartoon and asked them to describe in one sentence what was going on in the picture. All 25 responses were different. Next the professor put his results into a computer program designed to determine how many grammatically correct sentences could be generated from only the words used in those 25 sentences. The result was 19.8 billion different possibilities.

Other computer calculations have shown that it would take 10 trillion years — 2,000 times the estimated age of the earth — to say all of the possible sentences in English that use exactly 20 words. From this it would be highly unlikely that any 20-word sentence you hear has ever been spoken before, and similar calculations could be made for sentences of different lengths. The number of creative possibilities within the grammar, then, is virtually infinite. And yet, when a fundamental principle of grammar is violated, the speaker does not have to run through a complicated series of analyses to figure it out. He knows instantly.

From an analysis of the input-output relationship of a speaker, it would not be possible for a human being to deduce the subtle and complex rules of the grammar he uses with such authority.

Therefore, the fundamental grammar is innate.

Universal grammar, that set of properties common to any natural language by biological necessity, is a rich and highly articulated structure with explicit restrictions on the kinds of operations that can occur, though it is easy enough to imagine ways we could violate them. Applying purely mathematical operations to sentences, we could come up with any number of possibilities, like reversing the word order of an entire sentence, or switching the last word and the first, which would not yield grammatical sentences. But this does not occur in natural languages. No language constructs a question by simply reversing the order of a declarative sentence, but why not? It would seem to be a simple and obvious solution to the problem, much simpler than the systems that are actually used.

What is the nature of the original state? Or what is human nature?

Looks like snow...

That does it... I'm outta here!

A bird does not have to be taught to sing a specific kind of call, or to know when it is time to migrate for the winter. There are many specific behaviors which emerge developmentally but cannot be attributed to learning in the sense that we usually use the term. Walking is an example. Almost all human children without certain relatively rare disabilities learn to walk within the first two years of their lives.

The way this behavior is acquired also plays out in familiar and standard ways, from moving the limbs to slithering to crawling to standing while holding and so forth.

Human beings do not have to be taught to cry when they are sad or to laugh when it is appropriate.

Sexual behavior also plays out its development in fairly standard and predictable patterns. It is not observable at birth, but unfolds at the appropriate time according to what must be a pre-determined plan that exists within the organism from birth.

Most would agree that the capacity for language is innate to some degree in humans. Chomsky believes that the basic grammar itself is innate, born in us, part of our genetic material. He believes that language has a center in the brain that is separate unto itself.

In this connection, the word "programmed" is often applied, perhaps misleadingly. "Programmed" is an active verb and raises the question who or what is taking the action; who has done the programming. This is another realm entirely and not part of Chomsky's discussion. It is also a particularly contemporary metaphor that draws parallels between humans and computers which may or may not be valid and may be objectionable to some who believe that the activity of computers is fundamentally and qualitatively different from the behavior of sentient beings. Without delving into the source of this genetic material, the instinctual programs that play themselves out in the development of the child, Chomsky attempts to establish by logic that these behaviors in humans are not learned but are innate.

Chomsky comes to his conclusion not primarily by observation, but by logic. Observation is the source of the basic elements of the discourse, such as the observation of how children learn language from extremely limited information, but Chomsky's main contribution follows from the logical processes that he applies to those observations, the questions he asks, the chains of deduction he follows, and his conclusions.

There are other areas of human activity that might be investigated in similar ways as part of looking into the essence of what it means to be human. Human expressions in music and the arts, in religion, ethics, social structures seem also to have their universal qualities which express themselves in various, but remarkably similar ways in diverse cultures around the world.

Chomsky on Skinner and Behaviorism

Skinner's Behaviorism is one area where Chomsky's views on linguistics and his political views clearly come together.

Skinner claims that human beings are blank slates, totally controlled by outside influences, their conditioning. He takes will from the individual and replaces it in the environment.

He says: **"As a science of behavior adopts the strategy of physics and biology, the autonomous agent to which behavior has traditionally been attributed is replaced by the environment -- the environment in which the species evolved and in which the behavior of the individual is shaped and maintained."** [B.F. Skinner, Beyond Freedom and Dignity]

 Skinner states that scientific analysis will someday prove all this, he states it as though "it is in the nature of scientific inquiry," that his conclusion that behavior is determined by external factors must someday be proven. He doesn't offer proof of this, but expects you to take his claims, cloaked in scientific-sounding jargon, on faith, never of course calling it faith...

Chomsky uncloaks Skinner's dogmatism by first stating it clearly...

"In support of his belief that science will demonstrate that behavior is entirely a function of antecedent events, Skinner notes that physics advanced only when it 'stopped personifying things' and attributing to them 'wills, impulses, feelings, purposes,' and so on. Therefore, he concludes, the science of behavior will progress only when it stops personifying people and avoids reference to 'internal states.' No doubt physics advanced by rejecting the view that a rock's wish to fall is a factor in its 'behavior,' because in fact a rock has no such wish."

I'm fine right here, thank you.

...and terminates Skinner in the plainest imaginable English:

"For Skinner's argument to have any force, he must show that people have will, impulses, feelings, purposes, and the like no more than rocks do. If people differ from rocks in this respect, then a science of human behavior will have to take account of this fact." [FRS]

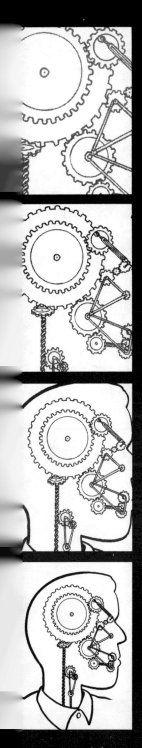

Chomsky has contributed greatly to refuting Behaviorism's ugly assertion that we are merely dull machines shaped by a history of reinforcement, exactly as free as rats in a maze, with no intrinsic needs other than physiological satiation.

Chomsky leans strongly toward the belief that human beings are not only born with an innate knowledge of grammar, but that we are also inclined by nature toward free creative inquiry and productive work.

Whether we live up to Chomsky's view of ourselves or down to Skinner's depends largely on whether we believe the lies we are told, or find ways to see through them.

If we don't see through them, we will be exactly as free as rats in a maze.

Which brings us to Chomsky's study of the media...

Noam Chomsky and the Media

Can You Believe What You See and Hear?

In order for democracy to be "democratic,"
the media has to fulfill two functions:

- The media must report the news fairly, completely, and without bias

- The media must function as a watchdog for the public against abuses of power

Noam Chomsky believes that the media fails miserably on both counts.

In Chomsky's view—which many of us feel instinctively—the mass media is little more than a public relations industry for the rich and powerful. Its function is to sell to the public rather than to inform them. Looking at it this way creates a more accurate picture of how the media work.

But what is it trying to sell us?

Necessary Illusions
The Science of Propaganda

In his book *Necessary Illusions*, Chomsky documents the history of propaganda, public relations, and other strategies of those who designate them-selves as having the right to control our thoughts and opinions without our conscious assent. He reminds us that although TV and print journalists constantly use buzzwords like "democracy," "capitalism," "freedom of speech," and

"equality," we rarely hear any discussion of what these words really mean or how they play out in our real lives. Chomsky not only takes us beyond the veil of propaganda, he also helps us see the flaws in our own thinking habits so that we can find the truth on our own. He does this with the rational precision of a great scientific mind and with the moral authority of a spiritual leader.

The subtitle of the book, **"Thought Control in Democratic Societies,"** is a typically explosive Chomskyan phrase, a collision of two concepts that are not normally encountered together in America. "Thought control" is something we associate with totalitarian countries: the Soviet Union, Nazi Germany, Cuba, etc. We call the United States a democracy, and in democracies everybody is free and equal.

We are free to think whatever we want and to read or watch or listen to whatever we want. To see the words **"thought control"** in connection with a democratic society seems strange.

Like any good scientist, Chomsky takes nothing for granted. He questions everything.

What is the function of communications media in a democratic society?

What kind of democracy do we want?

And what do we mean by democracy?

To answer these questions, Chomsky goes back to the founding of the American republic. There are two fundamentally opposing views in America of what democracy is, and of what freedom of the press is.

One notion of the role of media in a democracy is typified by the view of Supreme Court Justice William Powell who wrote that democracy requires free access to information.

"No individual can obtain for himself the information needed for the intelligent discharge of his political responsibilities..." said Powell. "By enabling the public to assert meaningful control over the political process, the press performs a crucial function in effecting the societal purpose of the First Amendment."

Within that definition of democracy citizens should "have the opportunity to inform themselves, to take part in inquiry and discussion and policy formation, and to advance their programs through political action."

This view is the standard belief in America.

But, unfortunately- according to Chomsky- it is not the way it really works.

The alternative view of the purpose of the media was expressed nicely by James Mill: The media's role is to "train the minds of the people to a virtuous attachment to their government." (That is so sinister that it bears repeating.)

... to "train the minds of the people to a virtuous attachment to their government."

(... and, adds Chomsky, "to the arrangements of the social, economic, and political order more generally." [NI])

In this view, democracy is only for an elite—and the media's job is to "train the minds of the people" to believe in the virtue of the elitist goons who rule them. This, says Chomsky, is more consistent with the ideas of the founding fathers as stated by John Jay who said that **"those who own the country should run it."**

"John Jay's maxim is, in fact, the principle on which the Republic was founded and maintained," says Chomsky, "and in its very nature capitalist democracy cannot stray far from this pattern...." [NI]

With this principle in operation, says Chomsky, politics becomes an interaction among groups of investors who compete for control of the state.

Edward Bernays, a leading figure in the rise of the public relations industry, said that persuasion is the very essence of the democratic process. *"A leader frequently cannot wait for the people to arrive at even general understanding ... Democratic leaders must play their part in ... engineering ... consent to socially constructive goals."*

("... engineering ... consent...")

Journalist Walter Lippman wrote in *Public Opinion* in 1921 that "the manufacture of consent" constituted a "revolution in the practice of democracy" and has become "a self conscious art and regular organ of popular government."

("... manufactur[ing] ... consent..."?)

"The common interests," said Lippman, "largely elude public opinion entirely, and can be managed only by a specialized class whose personal interests reach beyond the locality."

In The Encyclopedia of Social Sciences, Harold Laswell cautioned against believing "democratic dogmatisms about men being the best judges of their own interests." The elite who designate themselves as rulers must be in a position to impose their will and if social conditions do not permit sufficient force to insure obedience, then "a whole new technique of control, largely through propaganda," is necessary because of the "ignorance and superstition [of] the masses."

Reinhold Niebuhr, whom Jimmy Carter cited as one of his main influences, was the source of the quote that Chomsky chose as his title. Because of the "stupidity of the average man," he

must be given "necessary illusions" and "emotionally potent oversimplifications" instead of the truth.

Historian Thomas Bailey, arguing to avoid demilitarization after World War II, said, "because the masses are notoriously short-sighted and generally cannot see danger until it is at their throats, our statesmen are forced to deceive them into an awareness of their own long-run interests. Deception of the people may in fact become increasingly necessary unless we are willing to give our leaders in Washington a freer hand."

To recap Chomsky's view...

DEMOCRACY

- Our leaders consider us too stupid to be the judges of our own best interests.
- They believe that Democracy is only for the elite—the rich and powerful.
- They believe that "those who own the country should run it."

POLITICS

- Politics is not about elections or democracy.
- Politics is an interaction among groups of investors who compete for control of the state (country, earth...universe).

MEDIA

- The mass media is little more than a public relations industry for the rich and powerful. The media's job is to "train the minds of the people" to believe in the virtue of the powerful goons who rule them.

The Targets of Propaganda

According to Chomsky the two targets of propaganda are:

1. The political class, which is roughly the 20 percent of the population that is educated, articulate, and is expected to play some role in decision making. Essentially, they function as social managers, so this group must be deeply indoctrinated. Their consent is important.

2. The other 80 percent is expected to take orders-to go along without thinking. And they are the ones who usually pay.

Though it has been clearly stated in public forums that it may be necessary to fool the public, it does not mean that the practitioners of the deception are always conscious of their deception:

"It is probable that the most inhuman monsters, the Himmlers and the Mengeles, convince themselves that they are engaged in noble and courageous acts."[NI]

We're here to bring you peace...

In the third world, the US often resorts to violence to "restore democracy," which in reality usually means whichever regime—no matter how brutal—most benefits US investors. In the US itself, a tradition of human rights still stands in the way of a free exercise of governmental force, so subtler techniques are employed: the manufacture of consent, manipulating public opinion with necessary illusions, covert operations that congress and the media ignore until they overflow into public awareness too far to avoid comment. Then they are treated as scandals, isolated incidents. A great deal of attention is paid to a public drama involving chosen fall guys, who may be pardoned after massively expensive public procedures, or may do some token prison time before coming out and retiring comfortably on pensions or hush money. Or perhaps, as in the cases of Oliver North and G. Gordon Liddy, they may parlay their notoriety into new careers as politicians or media figures.

One "scandal" after another emerges and then passes out of public attention until the next incident. Each of these incidents is portrayed as an aberration, a misadventure that departs from the norm of high integrity and dedication to constitutional principles of the majority of our public officials. But many of us suspect that the "scandals" are really business as usual, the true operations of government occasionally poking through the blanket of necessary illusions.

The public wearies of it all, their senses battered with so much meaningless input. They may sense that it is bogus, but they feel they have no power to do anything about it.

The Threat of Democracy

In 1975 the Trilateral Commission published a study entitled "The Crisis of Democracy," on "the governability of democracies." The paper interpreted public participation in decision-making as a threat, which it is to the elite governing class. The media, it

says, are a "notable new source of power," that has contributed to "an excess of democracy" and a resulting "reduction in governmental authority." If journalists don't impose "standards of professionalism," says the study, "the alternative could well be regulation by the government."

The media is a "guided market system"—guided by profit

The media is a "guided market system"—guided by profit. And guided by the government. Which often amounts to the same thing. Information that is "guided" to suit an agenda—political or financial—is propaganda.

Propaganda is not the media's only function, but it is a large part of it. And—to state the obvious—nothing will appear within the media system that contradicts the purposes of the owners.

Or, to put it another way: **Ownership determines content.**

The question is, How exactly do the owners of our media "guide" its content without being heavyhanded about it? After all, if the owners of our media posted signs saying, "Anyone who reports news critical of our Magnificent Corporation or overly sympathetic to the working class will be fired, shot, or imprisoned," even in a society as passive as we've become, a few of us might lose our heads and strongly object.

How do the owners of our media control its content while managing to remain, for all intents and purposes, invisible?

"Never mind what's going on behind that curtain..."

The Propaganda Model

In *Manufacturing Consent,* Chomsky and co-author Edward S. Herman sketch out what they call a "propaganda model," describing the "invisible" forces that insure that the mass media will play the role of propagandists, transmit biased information instead of news, and do their masters' bidding without even being asked. The media, say Chomsky and Herman, merely "mobilize support for the special interests that dominate the state and private activity, and ... their choices, emphases, and omissions can often be understood best ... by analyzing them in such terms."[MC]

The heart of Chomsky's and Herman's propaganda model consists of what they call "news filters"- five of them. These filters, one level at a time, remove all "undesirable elements" from ever finding their way into your living room...or your mind.

Filter 1. Money: The great wealth of the owners, the fact that ownership of the media is concentrated in a few huge corporate hands, and the fact that media corporations, like other corporations, exist only to make a profit.

Filter 2. Advertising as their primary source of income.

Filter 3. Reliance on information provided by government, business, and "experts."

Filter 4. "Flak" as a means of disciplining the media.

Filter 5. "Anti communism" as a national religion and control mechanism.

(When the Soviet system collapsed, so did Filter 5; see explanation below for our attempts to find a new Evil Empire.)

FILTER 1. ONLY THE WEALTHY NEED APPLY

In the early 19th Century, a free press took root in England that represented the interests and identity of working people in a way that had been unknown before, but by mid-century the small papers had pretty much died out and were replaced by much larger entities.

83

As the market for newspapers grew and the technological requirements of publishing evolved, the cost of competing in that larger market also (to say the least) grew.

In 1837, the cost of establishing a profitable national weekly paper in England was under 1,000 pounds, with a break-even circulation of 6,200. By 1867 the estimated start-up cost of a London daily paper was 50,000 pounds. By the 1920s in America, newspaper companies were selling at from $6,000,000 to $18,000,000. [1]

The cost to enter today's media markets makes those amounts seem like a school child's lunch money.

The first "filter"—the massive financial requirement—is an enormous hurdle for anyone wishing to establish a place in the media market. Only the wealthy—the enormously wealthy—need apply.

---

1. James Curran and Jean Seaton. *Power Without Responsibility: The Press and Broadcasting in Britain.* 1985.

And every year the media is concentrated in fewer and fewer hands.

Q: HOW MANY MEDIA SYSTEMS/COMPANIES EXIST?

According to The Media Monopoly, written by Ben Bagdikian in **1982**, there were approximately **1,500** daily newspapers, **11,000** magazines, **9,000** radio stations, **1,500** TV stations, **2,400** book publishers and **seven** major movie studios in the United States, over **25,000** media organs in all. Many of these are small, with very limited coverage and receive all but their local news coverage from larger media and wire services.

Q: WHAT ABOUT THE MAJOR MEDIA?

The 29 largest media systems account for over half of the output of newspapers, and most of the magazines, radio, books, and movies. Bagdikian calls this elite group "a new Private Ministry of Information and Culture that can set national agenda."

Ownership is growing increasingly concentrated: In 1982, Bagdikian said 50 corporations controlled most of the major media outlets in the US. By the fourth edition of the book in 1993, the number was down to 20 and still dropping.

Q: WHAT IS THE "MEDIA OF INFLUENCE?"

The "Media of Influence" refers to highest tier of the media in terms of prestige, resources and coverage. It is made up of about 10-24 companies who, along with government wire services, define the national news agenda as well as providing the news itself for most of the lower level media companies.

The top tier (in 1986) included:

The three television networks:

- ABC (through its parent, Capital Cities)
- CBS
- NBC (General Electric)

The leading newspaper empires:

- The New York Times
- Washington Post
- Los Angeles Times (Times-Mirror)
- Wall Street Journal (Dow Jones)

- Knight-Ridder
- Gannett
- Hearst
- Scripps-Howard
- Newhouse (Advance Publications)
- The Tribune Company

Major news and general-interest magazines:

- Time
- Newsweek (Washington Post)
- Reader's Digest
- TV Guide (Triangle)
- U.S. News & World Report

A major book publisher:

- McGraw Hill.

Major cable TV systems:

- Murdoch
- Turner
- Cox
- General Corp.
- Taft
- Storer
- Group W (Westinghouse).

These 24 companies are owned by even larger corporations. Their main purpose is to maximize profits. They are owned by very wealthy people. All but one of the top companies have assets in excess of $1 billion.

Centralization of ownership of the top tier of media increased substantially after World War II, with the rise of television and its national networking. Before TV, news markets were local, though they depended on the top tiers for national and international news. Television is now the main source of news for the public.

But with the rise of cable TV, the market has fragmented somewhat, creating a trend toward decentralization. New electronic media, from on-line services to faxes and modems, may continue the trend toward decentralization, but the monopolists are hard at work finding ways to tie up the new media as they develop.

As we approach the end of the 20th Century, money still rules the media.

FILTER 2. ADVERTISING, THE LICENSE TO DO BUSINESS

Not another advertiser?!?

Before the rise of advertising, the price of a newspaper had to cover its cost of production. But with advertisers to pay the bills, a publication could be marketed at less than the cost to make it. This put papers that do not sell advertising out of the market.

Q: HOW / WHY DOES THAT DISTORT THE NEWS?

Advertising distorts the news because it makes a publication accountable to its advertisers more than to its readers. Media with an advertising subsidy can undercut the prices of media without and can then pick up the market of the low income readers as well. More revenue increases the ability to compete, to produce, to promote.

Advertisers learned early on that advertising in publications that cater to the affluent will make them more money because the affluent have money to spend. Publications that represent the interests and support the world view of the working class are at a disadvantage in the advertising competition because their readers are of modest means.

When the British social-democratic paper The Daily Herald went out of business in the 1960s, it actually had almost **double the readership** of The Times, the Financial Times and the Guardian **combined**. Its readers, according to surveys, were more loyal to it and read more of it than readers of the other papers. What it lacked was advertising. Some analysts believe the death of the Herald contributed to the diminishing fortunes of the Labor Party because there was no longer an alternative frame of reference by which to analyze events.

American broadcast media programming, as well as print media, is bought and sold by the advertisers. And they are not shy about controlling it.

Example:

Gulf and Western pulled its funding from public TV station WNET in 1985 when it ran a documentary called "Hungry For Profit," which criticized the activities of multinational corporations in the third world. A source at WNET said they anticipated a negative reaction to the program, and "did all we could to get the program sanitized." Apparently, they didn't **"sanitize"** it enough: Gulf and Western's CEO complained to the station that the program was "virulently anti-business if not anti-American," and said that WNET's behavior was not that of "a friend." According to the London Economist, "Most people believe that WNET would not make the same mistake again." (One of the great "filters" in corporations of every kind is, either you learn to read your boss's mind or you're out of a job.)

Programs that raise concerns over environmental or human rights issues that are consequences of the corporate system are not likely to be well-received at any network, even on public TV.

Television networks know what will sell to their advertisers and what won't. You don't have to be a rocket scientist to figure out that programs that create doubt over the way big business operates probably won't sell to your large corporate sponsors. Sponsors also object to programming that discusses disturbing and complex issues  that may disrupt the "buying mood." TV audiences are not thought of as "citizens" but as "consumers." Sponsors want "entertainment" that will offend the fewest possible and create no disturbance.

The primary purpose of the media from the standpoint of those who own it is to sell—and at the same time to protect their interests.

FILTER 3. WHERE THE NEWS COMES FROM. RELIANCE ON INFORMATION PROVIDED BY GOVERNMENT, BUSINESS, AND "EXPERTS."

In order to fill daily quotas for news material, the institutions of news media need steady reliable sources of news information. Reporters cannot be everywhere at once waiting for news stories to break so they concentrate their activities in places where news is breaking every day routinely, places like the White House, the Pentagon, the halls of Congress. Big business leaders are also credible sources for news stories. Information from these sources does not have to be checked or backed up, it is deemed credible by virtue of who it comes from.

This saves a lot of time, costly research and fact-checking. The news bureaucracies have an affinity with governmental and business bureaucracies and rely on them to satisfy their needs for a steady flow of news at low cost.

Many government agencies are terrifyingly helpful when it comes to supplying us with news: The Pentagon has a public information operation that employs thousands of people and spends hundreds of millions of dollars a year.

It is much larger than all the dissenting information sources put together.

Similar forces are in operation on local levels, with city hall and the police department as regular reporter beats.

CLEANS!
WHITENS!
BRIGHTENS!

NEWS

Government bureaucracies cater to the needs of news organizations, creating symbiotic relationships by making the work of gathering news easier, less expensive, government-sanctioned, and corporate-blessed.

Who cares if it's been "sanitized" to get through all those filters?

Besides, if you doubt the "official government version" of the news, you can always consult the experts. Of course, experts can be co-opted by big corporate or government interests, by funding them, sponsoring them, putting them on payrolls.

EXPERT

A study done on the MacNeil-Lehrer News Hour from January '85 to January '86 showed a breakdown into categories of the "experts" who appeared on the show. 40 percent were government officials or former government officials. Almost 12 percent were from conservative think tanks, 10 percent from the academic community, 2.5 percent were consultants and 4.2 percent were foreign government officials. Journalists made up 25.8 percent of the total. Not counting journalists, the percentage of government and former government officials was 54 percent.

In other words, the "experts" are recruited from the same "official sources" that "leaked" the news in the first place.

FILTER 4. FLAK

'Flak' is a cute insider's word for negative reactions to media statements in the form of letters, phone calls, petitions, lawsuits, speeches, congressional bills, and other forms of punitive action. At a certain point, flak can make it very difficult for an organ of media to function.

The capacity to generate flak that is truly threatening is proportional to power. The powerful can generate flak directly, such as letters or phone calls from the White House to anchormen or producers, demands from the FCC to produce documents related to a specific program, or threats from ad agencies or big sponsors to pull advertising or to sue. The powerful can create flak indirectly by complaining against the media to its employees and stockholders, generating advertising or press that denigrates the media, funding right wing monitoring or think tank operations that attack the media, or funding political campaigns of candidates who support their policies and will take a hard line toward media deviation.

In the '70s and '80s the corporate community sponsored the American Legal Foundation, the Capital Legal Foundation, the Media Institute, the Center for Media and Public Affairs, and Accuracy in Media (AIM), all institutions whose basic purpose is to produce flak against disobedient media.

The Media Institute sponsors media monitoring projects, conferences, and studies of the media which focus primarily on the failure of the media to accurately portray business and to give sufficient weight to the business point of view. It underwrites such works as John Corry's expose of alleged left-wing bias of the media. The chairman of the board in 1985 was Steven V. Seekins, the top public relations official of the American Medical Association. The chairman of the National Advisory Council was Herbert Schmertz of the Mobil Oil Corporation. The Center for Media and Public Affairs was created in the mid-'80s as a "nonprofit, non partisan" research institute and was praised by Patrick Buchanan, Faith Whittlesey and President Reagan. The Center's journal *The Media Monitor* keeps an eye on the alleged liberal and anti-business bias of the media. (One of the great ironies of the media is that despite the fact that these pro-business, pro-government, pro-status-quo "filters" give the media a frighteningly right-wing bias, it is constantly accused of left-wingery.)

Founded in 1969, Accuracy in Media (AIM)'s income grew from $5,000 in 1971 to $1.5 million in the early '80s, mostly donations from large corporations, foundations and heirs to the wealth of the corporate system. The sponsors are a wide range of large corporations including at least eight oil companies. AIM puts pressure on the media to follow the corporate agenda and a right-wing foreign policy.

FILTER 5. ANTI COMMUNISM

In 1988, the Soviet Union fell, forcing a rewrite of America's national obsession with anti communism as the central noble cause, the one unquestioned value in our culture other than making money.

Though the United States was founded on revolution, in our time the word revolution has become identified with an evil menace. The revolutions of Russia, China, and Cuba were extremely threatening to the ruling elites because communism would undermine their superior class status. It became the malevolent presence by which everything was justified. Communism gave the population an enemy against which to mobilize. Richard Nixon's first two political offices, as congressman and senator were gained by defeating incumbents who were taken by surprise and unable to defend themselves against his false accusations that they were communists. Though the charges were never substantiated, the fear and doubt created by Nixon's smear campaigns lasted long enough to get him into office. Eventually that tactic ran dry, but anti-communism remained the center of American political ideology until the fall of the Soviet Union.

After the fall of the Soviet Union there was some confusion from the propaganda experts on what enemy would be worthy of taking the place of the Evil Empire. Saddam Hussein served the purpose briefly, but a more reliable and malleable image has been that of Islamic fundamentalists, Muslims or Middle Easterners in general, who are portrayed as rabid extremists and terrorists as a general cultural trait.

CONCISION — THE STATE OR QUALITY OF BEING CONCISE.

"Concision" is the name news media professionals give to the principle of cutting everything to a bare minimum in order to make it fit within the format of "news."

The idea that all news has to fit into this kind of format is an unquestioned assumption. The format was established in the early days of American television. It is structured around "commercial breaks" every few minutes as required by "our sponsors" who pay for the programming.

The commercial breaks are about a third of all viewing time. It is impossible for anyone on our mass media to go into any issue at length. According to Jeff Greenfield, producer of "Nightline," **"It makes about as much sense for us to have someone on 'Nightline' who takes six minutes to answer a question as it does to have someone who doesn't speak English."**[MCF]

Through the principle of concision, it is assured that only conventional ideas will pass through the media filter, because ideas that everyone knows by heart require no support. When you say the Soviet Union invaded Afghanistan, no one will challenge you. But if you say that the US invaded Vietnam, you will be required to justify it.

Most Americans have never considered the US action in Vietnam an invasion. Yet, according to Chomsky, it was an invasion in precisely the same way that the invasion of Afghanistan was an invasion. But this runs counter to the premises that dominate the American news media. It is not part of the American vocabulary.

KEEPING IN LINE

Within the media system, the herd instinct assures that the proper point of view is maintained. Reporters do not have to consciously distort the news. If they adopt the "correct" world view, they will write as they are supposed to write.

Whoever writes for a newspaper must write in the editorial voice of that paper. Whatever deviates too far will be cut out. Whoever ignores the rules will not long be a part of the institution. And make no mistake— there are rules. And they're more strictly enforced than most drug or traffic laws. The proof is in the publication.

DON'T TAKE CHOMSKY'S WORD FOR IT—CHECK IT OUT FOR YOURSELF

A wonderful example of Chomsky's unique combination of scientific objectivity and common sense simplicity is the way he gauges the importance (to the media) of one story compared to another. It's so simple it's brilliant: He actually measures the amount of column space devoted to coverage of different subjects as compared to the amount of coverage given to other similar subjects.

You can apply that method in a variety of ways:

Which story does this newspaper/magazine consider most important? (...and is there a pattern on which kind of stories they focus on and those they underplay?)

How does newspaper "A" compare to newspaper "B," "C," "D"...?

(One way you learn which newspapers and periodicals to "trust" is to see if they spend the most column space on the subjects you consider most important.)

The technique works as well with TV news-you just measure minutes of broadcast time devoted to each subject. Try it; it's a real eye-opener to see what a TV network's "values" really are; and to see (for example) the enormous difference in emphasis between a TV network largely owned by a corporation that manufactures weapons, compared to one that's affiliated with a food-and-tobacco conglomerate (or to one whose CEO is famous for donating enormous sums of money to Israel). The "news" is very personal and can be "adjusted" to fit the needs of whoever owns it.

Those who wish to remain employed, to maintain the prestige of working for an important paper, to keep their employment resumes blemish-free will tow the line.

"Case by case, we find that conformity is the easy way, and the path to privilege and prestige; dissidence carries personal costs," [CR]

We began this section on Media with an awakening, a realization, a truth...

The media's function is NOT to inform the public, it is to SELL to the public.

That truth led to a question...

But what is it is trying to sell us?

As we have seen, our media has done a fine job of selling us the notion that we the people run our own country, that we are, in some meaningful sense, a democracy.

To that end, it has sold us a few perfectly ridiculous fantasies:

FANTASY 1: Our country is not owned, run, and controlled by a handful of rich people.

FANTASY 2: Our media are not owned, run, and controlled by a handful of rich people.

FANTASY 3 (the most dangerous of all) **:** Our opinions are freely formed, not coerced, conned, or manufactured in accordance with the designs of a handful of rich people.

But there is something we have left out. There is another thing that our media works hard to sell us: a fake history that leaves out the major players and bears little resemblance to reality. As usual, Chomsky doesn't beat around the bush:

"Why is it that the propaganda system is geared to suppressing any inquiry into... the role of corporations in foreign policy...?"

"Why such efforts to conceal the real history with fables about the awesome nobility of our intentions, flawed only by blunders arising from our naivete and simpleminded goodness...?"

"I think there is a good reason why the propaganda system works that way. It recognizes that the public will not support the actual policies.

This is not a pipe

Therefore it is important to prevent any knowledge or understanding of them."[CR.]

This is not a policy

What is that history that is so ugly that it must be concealed by fables?

What are those policies that we would not support if we were aware of?

What exactly are those policies that our government so carefully hides?

Chomsky on Politics

F or the sake of clarity and convenience, this book divides Media and Politics into separate chapters—but the point of the book is that they are inseparable.

Nothing better illustrates that point than the story of a little book called **Counter-Revolutionary Violence.**

In 1973, Claude McCaleb, publisher of Warner Modular books, decided that Watergate was merely a symptom of America's overall deterioration, so he planned to publish a series of books exploring his idea. One of the books in the series was an ornery little book called **Counter-Revolutionary Violence**—written by Noam Chomsky and Edward S. Herman: "Their thesis was that the United States, in attempting to suppress revolutionary movements in underdeveloped countries, had become the leading source of violence against native people." (*The Media Monopoly*—Ben H. Bagdikian)

When William Sarnoff, the president of **all** Warner books...

Let us pause momentarily for station identification: Warner Modular books (which was preparing to publish the Little Book) was a subsidiary of Warner **Publications** (which was a subsidiary of Warner **Communications**) (which owned factories in West Germany and Brazil and had "considerable interests" in books, movies, broadcasting, video games, and Richard Nixon).

When William Sarnoff, the president of **all** Warner books, learned that a company under his spiritual guidance was preparing to advertise, print, and publish the Chomsky-Herman book, he brutally chewed out Mr. McCaleb, canceled the ads, ordered the destruction of the catalogues announcing the book, halted the printing, and destroyed any books that had been printed.

Freedom of speech doesn't have a chance against Politics, Media, & Money.

When you hear the report of the day's news,

do you often get the feeling that it doesn't "compute,"

it doesn't quite make sense... like something was left out?

The media left out *lots* of stuff about me personally, but all that soon changed with...

...ME! They nailed my fannie to the wall every chance they got, and I never forgave them for it.

When Chomsky explains what the media leaves out, suddenly the news-of-the-day makes perfect sense. Sometimes the media leaves out specific things (we'll get to those later), but even more insidious (because it affects the way we see **everything**), they leave out entire concepts, without which our world makes no sense. One of the concepts that has been pretended out of existence by our

media is the reality that the Western "Democracies" (America included) are **still** divided into the **Royalty** and the **Peasants**, the **Rulers** and the **Ruled**...

In place of that reality, they feed us ...

The Myth of the Classless Society

There is a body of folklore that reaches all the way back through our history, about America being a country where people are not separated into social and economic classes, a place where everyone is truly free and equal. (If you believe that, there's a big white house in Washington, DC we'd like to sell you.) Once we had kings; before that we may have had packleaders. The layers of social classes included peasants, merchants, landed gentry, nobles, aristocracy and royalty. Today we have presidents, prime ministers, dictators, managers, officers, owners. Only the names have changed. No matter what you call it, the world is still divided into Us and Them.

What should we call today's rulers? Think about that for a moment while we give America credit for the good place that it thought about becoming...

In the U.S. since the '60s, the trend has been a shrinking middle class, wealth concentrated into fewer and fewer hands, and a general decrease in economic prosperity and quality of life for the vast majority. Those who drop from the middle class are forced to tighten their belts drastically, but for the growing underclass of people who are no longer participants in the economic system, it means a brutal struggle for day-to-day survival.

It is no longer possible to pretend we are a classless society.

Holding on to such symbols is choosing to be blind.

So what do we call today's rulers? They may not be genealogical heirs to yesterday's aristocracy (though in many cases they are), but they are certainly the historical heirs of the aristocracies. And they intend to rule.

To many, the phrase "ruling class" would sound too much like

Marxism or, God forbid, communism. Whatever you call them, today's rulers get very nervous when you shine a flashlight on them. They know the power of the media. Some people prefer to think there are no rulers and to put the question out of their minds. But if it has crossed your mind that perhaps all Americans are not equal -- not before the law and certainly not in terms of the benefits we receive from the government -- then you have already recognized that there are ranks in society.

And if that is so, then there is, by definition, an elite. If that word is offensive, too Marxian or too something, then replace it with whatever word pleases you: bosses, big guys, operators, upper class, masters, whatever.

(Or, if you choose, stick your head back in the sand, give them no name, and continue to pretend they don't exist.)

But if we are going to talk about them—which we are—we have to call them something. Rulers is as good a word as any.

Who Are These Rulers?

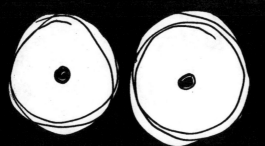

They are investment bankers, boards of directors, government officeholders. The center of world power is in America, but it is not by any means exclusively American. It is an international elite. It is the aristocracy of the modern world. The insiders operate mostly in secret while orchestrating distracting movements on the stage of politics. They are extremely powerful and extremely skilled at what they do.

But they are not all-powerful.
They are only human.

In the dictatorships of the third world, the rulers can do practically whatever they please. But inside the U.S. there is still a large measure of per-

sonal freedom. The rulers are a tiny minority. What they fear most is that the sleeping giant, the public—the people—will wake up and take control of what Orwell called "the space

between the ears" and actually use the power it doesn't know it has. That's why the rulers put so much effort and money into propaganda.

They know if the public ever gets hip to their game, they are finished.

As large and overwhelming as the system of control is, it is created by human beings and is not omnipotent. It grows naturally from the logic of history, from the time when aristocracies dominated, and from the state/business partnerships of colonialism.

Partly out fear, partly out of cowardice, mainly out a sense of entitlement

...they rig every game they play.

And from greed.

Welfare for the Rich

The Hoax Of The Free Market System

Help the Mansionless

In America "The Free Market System" is treated as a sacred principle. All economic problems are said to be cured by the functioning of the "free market" which, through natural competition, will cause the best products and the best prices to prevail for the betterment of all. The free market always makes the best choices and will fashion the most perfect society. But a closer look at how the economic system functions, who pays the taxes and how tax money is spent, who gets subsidized and who doesn't, reveals that the free market system is only a theory—it does not exist in reality.

In its place, a complex system of tax laws, government manipulation of public money, regulations, and various other magic tricks insure that certain businesses will thrive regardless of whether the free market will support them or not.

In other words, the free-market system is a hoax.

The U.S. economy, to put it bluntly, is rigged.

The idea of the free market is fine for economics textbooks and for hyping the masses, but real planners have not taken it seriously for a long time. That's why the government subsidizes certain industries. But it is not done openly. The subsidies, often massive, are disguised in various ways, mostly through "defense" programs, which take half of every tax dollar; also through subtleties in the tax structure that channel the tax money where the masters want it to go.

Welfare for the Rich—How It Works

During his first year in office, Clinton spoke to workers at the Boeing Company, telling the "cheering throng" that Boeing "is a model for companies across America" and the prime example of the "new vision of American relations with Asia," where "China alone now buys one of every six of [Boeing's] planes." At the same time Clinton announced a decision to sell Cray supercomputers to China in violation of congressional legislation. [NCZM]

The examples Clinton used to celebrate the success of the free market system are laughable. The aircraft and computer industries were founded (and still rely) on huge taxpayer subsidies—Welfare for the Rich. Boeing and Cray supercomputers would be lucky to survive if it weren't for enormous government subsidies. Agriculture is also protected and subsidized. High technology industries have been funded through the Pentagon's generous Welfare System since the late 1940s.

Since World War Two, there has been a program of suburbanizing America that, says Chomsky,

"Under the cover of defense, established the modern motor and air transport industries as core elements of the economy, with a cost to the public that goes far beyond the tens of billions of taxpayer dollars used in this massive government social engineering project...." [NCZM]

The Federal Highway Acts of 1944, 1956, and 1968, funneled billions of taxpayer dollars into a national highway system that was the brainchild of Alfred Sloan, chairman of GM. It made the American economy dependent on gasoline-powered transportation and gave the oil industry a virtual energy monopoly. This dependency would lead eventually to events like the Gulf War, in which hundreds of thousands of Iraquis were killed to ensure U.S. control of Middle Eastern oil.

The suburbanization of America was not the result of free market forces producing the most competitive products. It was engineered by the corporations that run our country. For example, between 1936 and 1949, National City Lines, a holding company sponsored and funded by General Motors, Firestone Rubber Company and Standard Oil of California, bought out more than 100 electric surface transit systems in 45 cities including New York, Philadelphia, and Los Angeles and dismantled them: They were replaced with GM buses. In 1949, GM and its partners were convicted in Federal District Court in Chicago of criminal conspiracy for this project and fined $5,000— not even a slap on the hubcap for General Motors!—but the effect was irreversible. The GM busses stayed and the electric street cars were history. (To get the full measure of the brutal irony of that slippery maneuver, virtually every GM auto show of the last 20 has featured electric cars—"the wave of the future.")

Arms sales to oil producing countries are a device used to sustain Boeing, a publicly-subsidized privately-run corporation that Clinton called the "model of the free market vision."

This is so beautiful...

**"Publicly _subsidized_," "government _subsidy_"...?
What exactly do those terms mean?
It's simple, really.**

**The word "subsidy,"
tacked on to the name of a large corporation,
is a euphemism
for <u>Welfare</u> <u>for</u> <u>the</u> <u>Rich</u>.**

These "government subsidies" maintain the system by which profits from oil production go to the U.S. and Britain, not to the people of the oil-producing region. Referring to the April 1977 efforts to sell Iran advanced armaments, The New York Times said that "one of the principal reasons behind the Pentagon pressure for the offer to Iran was to keep the Boeing production line open."

When Secretary of State James Baker and President George Bush intervened in a secret meeting in October 1989 to ensure Saddam Hussein another $1 billion in loan guarantees (though the Treasury and Commerce departments had said that Iraq was not creditworthy), it was for the same purpose. Gassing of Kurds and torture of dissidents were non-issues. The State Department insisted that the additional billion for Saddam was justified because Iraq was "very important to U.S. interests in the Middle East," was "influential in the peace process," and "a key to maintaining stability in the region, offering great trade opportunities for U.S. companies."

You've been a very bad boy, Saddam... here's a billion dollars... now go play.

"Apart from maintaining a particular form of 'stability' in the interests of the world rulers, the Pentagon must continue to provide lavishly for Newt Gingrich and his rich constituents by means of a taxpayer subsidy to advanced industry. Nothing has changed in this regard since the early post-war period, when the business world recognized that the aircraft industry, established by public funds and wartime profiteering, 'cannot satisfactorily exist in a pure, uncompetitive, unsubsidized, "free enterprise" economy' [Fortune] and that 'the government is their only possible savior' [Business Week]. [2]

[2] [NCZM]

Uncle Newt's Double-Standard

Newt Gingrich's "Contract with America" is a program designed to take advantage of the double-standard of the "free market": public subsidy for the rich—free market discipline for the poor. Uncle Newt's agenda seeks cuts in social spending, including education, low income housing, rent subsidies (what they sneeringly call "entitlements"), denying aid to children of "minor mothers" and those on welfare —while increasing Welfare for the Rich.

"The principles are clear and explicit. Free markets are fine for the third world and its growing counterpart at home. Mothers with dependent children can be sternly lectured on the need for self-reliance, but not dependent executives and investors, please. For them, the welfare state must flourish." [3][my emphasis]

Welfare for the Rich comes in an endless variety of forms, including "entitlements" like capital gains cuts, investment subsidies, increased tax exemptions for estates, reduced health and safety regulations, larger allowances for depreciation and, of course, the Mother of All Entitlements, "increased military expenditures"—already the largest item on the budget by far.

[3] "The Clinton Vision: An Update," Z magazine, 1994

116

"National Defense" says Chomsky, "is a sick joke. The U.S. faces no threats, and already spends more on `defense' than the entire world combined." [4]

Hey there big fella... ever think about cutting back a little...?

USA
$ $ $ $

"The United States developed its own economy behind very high protectionist walls with enormous state intervention and it maintains it that way. The Pentagon system, for example, is itself a huge government program arranged for a taxpayer subsidy to advanced industry. I can't imagine anything more radically opposed to the free market." [INT]

If the U.S. faces no threats
yet spends more on "defense" than
the entire world combined
what, you may wonder,
does the Pentagon spend all
that friggin' money on?

[4] "Rollback Part 1" a report on the '94 elections," by N.C. in *Z* magazine, Jan. 1995

Neo Colonialism...
Friendly Dictators...
Client States...
In other words ...

We Spread Democracy!

Colonialism—THEN and NOW

The structure of power that operates in the world today is a direct descendant of historical colonialism. The systems that control us today are merely refined versions of the control systems that forced colonial natives into submission 500 years ago. Or, to be more precise—since the ruling elite never do their own dirty work—the systems that control us today, are the systems that manipulated, conned, or coerced the powerless citizens of one country to force the powerless citizens of another country into submission, colonialism, and slavery.

I'll take "Historical Colonialism" for one hundred, Alex...

Economist Adam Smith, the patron saint of the free market ideology, wrote in 1776 that "the discovery of America and that of the passage to the East Indies by the Cape of Good Hope are the two greatest and most important events in the history of mankind..."

Smith honestly believed that the "new set of exchanges"—of ideas, of culture, of trade, of human energy and ingenuity—would benefit both the Old World and the New.

It didn't take him long to realize that he was very wrong:

I was very wrong...

A. SMITH

"The savage injustice of the Europeans rendered an event, which ought to have been beneficial to all, ruinous and destructive to several of those unfortunate countries. To the natives ... both of the East and West Indies, all the commercial benefits which can have resulted from those events have been sunk and lost in the dreadful misfortunes which they have occasioned."

What was it that gave the Europeans the better end of the deal? **"Superiority of force,"** said Smith, with which **"they were able to commit with impunity every sort of injustice in those remote countries."**

Who was calling whom "savages"?

But those were the bad old days.

In those days, even the good guys were rotten.

People weren't civilized like we are now, right?

FOREIGN POLICY: Friendly Dictators & Client States

In 1979, Chomsky and Edward Herman wrote a book called *The Washington Connection and Third World Fascism*, which describes the military take-overs of 18 Latin American countries between 1960 and 1978. The book presents enough evidence to convince anyone with the guts to read it that the U.S. government was a major player in every one of those military take-overs.

U.S. "foreign policy"—which is impossible to comprehend if you believe the media baloney spreaders—clearly did have a pattern.

But it had nothing to do with spreading democracy.

In country after country, not only in Latin America, but in Iran, Greece, the Philippines, and Indonesia to name a few, the U.S. supported brutal, democracy-repressing military dictatorships, in the interest of establishing and protecting "client states."

Chomsky and Herman define "client states:"

"The basic fact is that the United States has organized under its sponsorship and protection a neo-colonial system of client states ruled mainly by terror, and serving the interests of a small local and foreign business and military elite. The fundamental belief, or ideological pretense, is that the United States is dedicated to furthering the cause of democracy and human rights throughout the world, though it may occasionally err in the pursuit of this objective."[WC]

The REAL New World Order— How It Started

The present world system crystallized after World War II when the United States found itself in a position of unprecedented power. The U.S. had escaped the widespread devastation of the war that had destroyed much of Europe, and the stimulus of the war had tripled American production. The U.S., naturally, left no scheme untried in its attempt to capitalize on its newfound power.

In 1948 **George Kennan**, a State Department planner, wrote Policy Planning Study 23, explaining the rationale behind the system of military "client states" that the U.S. has maintained since World War II.

The document said "we have about 50 percent of the world's wealth, but only about 6 percent of its population ... In this situation we cannot fail to be the object of envy and resentment. Our real task in the coming period is to devise a pattern of relationships that will permit us to maintain this disparity ... To do so we will have to dispense with sentimentality and daydreaming; and our attention will have to be concentrated everywhere on our immediate national objectives... We should cease to talk about vague and ... unreal objectives such as human rights, the raising of living standards and democratization."

I'll be the envy of the free world wearing this...

In a 1950 briefing of U.S. ambassadors to Latin American countries, Kennan warned the diplomats that they must guard against the spreading of the dangerous idea "that governments are responsible for the well being of their people." In order to combat this idea, Kennan said, "we should not hesitate before police repression by the local government... It is better to have a strong regime in power than a liberal one if it is indulgent and relaxed and penetrated by Communists."

Anyone who had the dangerous idea that governments were responsible for their people was considered a Communist by U.S. top guns.

The REAL Objective Of The New World Order

It was simple, really: America had only 6 percent of the world's population—but 50 percent of the world's wealth. If it wanted to keep it's advantage—or better yet increase it!—America had to force the rest of the world to accept its dominance. Of course, keeping the edge in wealth would be increasingly difficult as countries rebuilt after the war and undeveloped countries began to industrialize.

Clearly, the only way it could be "maintained" was the same way that colonialism was "established" in the first place...

THROUGH BRUTE FORCE.

(Is the news beginning to make a bit more sense now?)

Torture

Brute force comes in many versions, one of the ugliest of which is torture. For the past 300 years (if you don't count blacks or women), torture had pretty much gone out of fashion in the West. Fashions change: A 1975 Amnesty International "Report on Torture" listed 26 countries that used torture "on an administrative basis" or as "an essential mode of governance."

Maybe it was just a coincidence, but except for their penchant for torture, the only thing that all 26 countries had in common was U.S. military aid, police training, and/or military personnel. Torture was

(and is) not only tolerated by American "interests," the U.S. government trains and equips people to do it.

It trains them very well...

After the U.S.-assisted military coup in Chile in 1973, Amnesty International went in to survey the damage. Amnesty's Report stated that "Many people were tortured to death by means of endless whipping as well as beating with fists, feet and rifle butts. Prisoners were beaten on all parts of the body, including the head and the sexual organs. The bodies of prisoners were found in the Rio Mapocho, sometimes disfigured beyond recognition."

What exactly are these "American interests" we keep hearing about?

It's simple: American interests are not <u>my</u> interests or <u>your</u> interests. American interests are American <u>corporations</u> that "own" the resources of other people's countries.

... if you ask, "How can you own the resources of another people's country? What gives you that right?"

... and if you realize that there can be only one answer: "Brute force."

... suddenly the news begins to make a little more sense.

American "corporate interests," backed by American military power, serving the interests of American investors, who "own" another country's resources...? To the natives of those countries, many with indigenous ancestors going back thousands of years, ownership of their land and resources by foreigners has questionable legitimacy (to say the least). When foreign ownership results in near slave-labor, oppressive working conditions, and the most wretched poverty, it cannot endure peacefully. Resistance is inevitable ... and expected ... and countered with the most brutal and repressive measures.

When native people decide that the profits from their countries' sources

should be directed toward their own countries and not toward the colonial masters,

they may try to institute reforms. They may call them "land reforms" or "nationalization of industries,"

but regardless of what the people believe or how righteous their claims are,

the U.S. calls them "communists" or "ultranationalists" or "extremists"

—bad names for bad people. Bad people deserve bad things.

Therefore, under that wonderfully convenient value system, the United States is justified in using the most extreme violence ... to "restore democracy"...

... because "Communism" is the great evil of the world. Communism, we are told, is the opposite of democracy, the opposite of freedom.

But whose freedom?

The freedom of the majority of the country itself?

Or the freedom of a few American investors?

In the Holy War against "Communism," our leaders justify the use of torture, terror, assassination, death squads...

**Do they have consciences?
Do they ever ask themselves ...
Why do so many people have to die
to protect "our way of life"?**

This aspect of American foreign policy—our widespread slaughter of and indifference to indigenous peoples—is not the sort of thing the media is likely to brag about.

> I can't see anything from here...

> I can't hear anything from here...

BACK TO YOU
IN THE
BOOTH

**But is that excuse enough to ignore it?
Aren't we, in some sense, obliged to witness it,
maybe even to act on it?**

"*These are not just academic exercises. We're not talking about the media on Mars or in the 18th Century. There are real human beings who are suffering and being tortured and starving because of policies we are involved in because we as citizens of a democratic society are involved in and directly responsible for the actions of our government. What the media are doing is ensuring that we don't act on our responsibilities.*" [MCF]

If you're offended, well...
Nobody ever said that
Chomsky was comforting.

Chomsky tells the truth.

HISTORY:
One Or Two Things They
Don't Tell You

Chomsky's version of history is different from the official history that appears in school textbooks or in *The New York Times*. The facts are the same in their broad strokes. But the interpretation of those facts is fundamentally different and there are many other facts that you would never read in The Times.

For example: what does *New York Times* reporter Leslie Gelb mean when she speaks of President Johnson's "swift, decisive and successful takeover and re-democratization of the Dominican Republic in 1965"?

In school you may have been taught that you were supposed to know your lessons already so you'd better not ask questions and reveal your ignorance.

But would it be too much to ask for something a little more specific about what "re-democratization" means?

Especially following the word "takeover."

What exactly went on there? In Chomsky's *Turning the Tide*, he gives a closer look than what appeared in the mainstream press. These facts can be verified if you are willing to go beyond the news that is pushed in your face every day. Information is available in many books and magazines besides the mass-market ones. Facts also slip through mainstream channels, but you have to read a variety of them and then put all the facts together to see the patterns the media insiders will most assuredly not point out to you.

For Example:

During the Kennedy administration, the Dominican Republic was owned by its president, Trujillo, and a handful of companies. Trujillo's

share was an estimated 65-85 percent of the country's economy, a larger share than his allies who were growing weary of him...so they sent some bad people to murder him. Crude dude that he was, he was an embarrassment to the

lofty rhetoric of the Kennedy administration...so Kennedy sent the CIA to murder him. It took awhile, and nobody's sure who pulled it off, but somebody managed to kill the greedy man.

In 1962, in the country's first free elections, **Juan Bosch** was elected president. Bosch introduced a democratic constitution

and legal system, attacked corruption, defended civil liberties, urged police restraint, slashed the salaries of high officials and refused the customary perks of office. Bosch's reforms went a long way toward helping his people.

Unfortunately, that angered U.S. "interests." After Bosch had been in office for seven months, the military overthrew him. The U.S. decided (as the American Ambassador put it) to "let him go." After going through the motions of objecting to the overthrow of a democratically elected government, the U.S. gave full support to the military regime. American interests, which had been temporarily threatened by democracy, were once again in safe hands.

Making The World Safe For Democracy

Corruption returned, the economy declined, and before you could say "American interests," the country was as impoverished

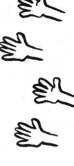

and corrupt as it had been before Bosch's reforms. However, nobody had anticipated the fact that the people of The Dominican Republic, having had a taste of democracy,

weren't going to let it go that easily. The people stood up for their rights, overthrew the brutal military-regime and moved toward restoring Bosch to power—and democracy to their country. It was almost a wonderful story. Almost.

The U.S. sent 23,000 American soldiers to help the corrupt military regime beat down the people of the Dominican Republic. Once again, the democratically elected government of the Dominican Republic was overthrown, the threat to U.S. business interests was removed, and the world was once again safe for greed.

The result, says Chomsky, was **"the usual one: death squads, torture, repression, an increase in poverty and malnutrition for the mass of the population, slave labor conditions, vast emigration, and outstanding opportunities for U.S. investors, whose control over the economy reached new heights."**[TT]

And newspapers throughout the country lauded President Johnson for sending 23,000 troops "to seek peace."

That (in case you were wondering) was not an isolated incident. It is typical of U.S. policy throughout the third world...

Guatemala

Jacobo Arbenz was elected president of Guatemala in 1951. His land reforms increased productivity, provided food and cash to the peasants, and involved them in the political system for the first time in 400 years. Unfortunately, Arbenz was too honorable to suit his American counterparts.

He tried to expropri-ate unused lands held by the United Fruit Company so that he could give the land to landless peas-ants. Arbenz, who was trying hard not to screw anybody, offered payment to United Fruit based on its fraudulent tax valuation. Eisenhower's Under-Secretary of

State, who was too "smart" to be fooled, said that Guatemala was playing "the commu-nist game" by allowing civil rights to communists. Under the pretext of stopping a commu-nist takeover, the good old CIA over-threw the democra-tically elected government of Guatemala and restored military rule.

"Land reform was repealed, its beneficiaries dispossessed, peasant cooperatives were dis-solved, the literacy program was halted, the econ-omy collapsed, the labor unions were destroyed and the killings began." [TT]

The killings, encouraged, sponsored, and paid for by the U.S., continued for years. The Guatemalan Conference of Bishops said that "never in our history have such extremes been reached, with the assassinations now falling into the category of genocide."

Chomsky on Nicaragua

A French priest and trainer of nurses in the north of Nicaragua testified to the World Court about a handicapped person murdered "for the fun of

it," of women raped, of a body found with the eyes gouged out, and a girl of 15 who had been forced into prostitution at a Contra camp in Honduras. He testified that the Contras cre-ated an atmosphere of terror through kid-napping, rape, murder and torture.

The Boston Globe did a 100-word story on this testimony.

The New York Times didn't report it.

"What the U.S.-run Contra forces did in Nicaragua or what our terrorist proxies do in El Salvador or Guatemala isn't only ordinary killing. A major element is brutal, sadistic torture -- beating infants against rocks, hanging women by their feet with their breasts cut off and the skin of their faces peeled back so they will bleed to death, chopping people's heads off and putting them on stakes. The point is to crush independent nationalism and popular forces that might bring about meaningful democracy." [WU.S.]

Chomsky on Noriega

"Noriega's career fits a standard pattern. Typically, the thugs and gangsters whom the U.S. backs reach a point in their careers when they become too independent and too grasping, outliving their usefulness. Instead of just robbing the poor and safeguarding the business climate, they begin to interfere with Washington's natural allies, the local business elite and oligarchy, or even U.S. interests directly. At that point, Washington begins to vacillate; we hear of human rights violations that were cheerfully ignored in the past, and sometimes the U.S. government acts to remove them, even to attempt to assassinate them, as in the case of Trujillo. By 1986-7, the only question was when and how Noriega should be removed..."[DD]

We will, we will, ROCK YOU!

Chomsky on The Middle East and "Terrorism"

Under the "New World Order" (which is exactly the same as the "Old World Order") it is necessary to ensure that the wealth of the oil reserves goes to the West, not to the Middle Eastern countries that produce the oil—and certainly not to the people who live in those countries.

This "arrangement"—like every situation in which "outside interests" manage to make enormous profits off of the resources of the indigenous people while the people themselves live in dire poverty—is virtually guaranteed to create perpetual unrest.

Since the Russian Revolution of 1917, the standard justification for virtually all U.S. policies was the threat of Communist expansion. Having lost that scapegoat now the government is trying to come up with a new scenario. Says Chomsky, **"In reality, the 'threat to our interests' in the Middle East as elsewhere, had always been indigenous nationalism, a fact stressed in internal documents and sometimes publicly."**

The Arab-Israeli conflict adds its own special problems. Israel, for its part, instigates and promotes conflict between the U.S. and Iran, the U.S. and Iraq, the U.S. and Syria—the U.S. and virtually every Arab, Muslim, or Middle Eastern country. Chomsky: "The propaganda campaign about 'Islamic fundamentalism' has its farcical elements -- even putting aside the fact that U.S. culture compares with Iran in its religious fundamentalism. The most extreme Islamic fundamentalist state in the world is the loyal U.S. ally Saudi Arabia, or to be more precise, the family dictatorship that serves as the 'Arab facade' behind which the U.S. effectively controls the Arabian peninsula."

Islamic fundamentalism is only a problem when it gets "out of control," and becomes radical "nationalism," or "ultra nationalism."

Terrorism. The definition used by American authorities and adopted obediently by the media boils down to: It's "terrorism" when they do it, not when we do. Torture, mutilation, bombs, men with bayonets herding families into barbed wire pens...

These are not things people like to think about.

The fact that we don't want to know about them makes them easy to hide.

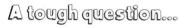

A tough question...

If atrocities, brutal murders, and other crimes against humanity were being committed or sponsored by agencies of your government

... would you want to know?

"To ask serious questions about the nature and behavior of one's own society is often difficult and unpleasant; difficult because the answers are generally concealed, and unpleasant because the answers are often not only ugly ... but also painful. To understand the truth about these matters is to be led to action that may not be easy to undertake and that may even carry a significant personal cost. In contrast, the easy way is to succumb to the demands of the powerful, to avoid searching questions, and to accept the doctrine that is hammered home incessantly by the propaganda system. This is, no doubt, the main reason for the easy victory of dominant ideologies, for the general tendency to remain silent or to keep fairly close to official doctrine with regard to the behavior of one's own state and its allies ... while lining up to condemn the real or alleged crimes of its enemies." [TNCW]

Question Everything ...

Not long before he was murdered, Martin Luther King, Jr. made a statement that struck many people as shocking:

"The greatest purveyor of violence is our own country."

Dr. King said it; Chomsky proves it. In book after book, Chomsky carefully documents dozens, if not hundreds, of examples of unbelievable atrocities directly attributable to the U.S.—and paid for by your tax money.

America's brutal "foreign policy" is an insult to every person who still has any semblance of conscience. It makes a mockery of everything the U.S. purports to stand for ... and, in the process, it has nearly succeeded in destroying the once-powerful U.S. economy.

Coming home to roost

Postwar America was the model for economic growth in an industrial society that was envied and emulated the world over. The American middle class grew throughout the '50s and into the '60s and this looked like the model for how capitalism could work, lifting the majority up with the prosperity it generated. At the same time just south of the Rio Grande, Mexico was the model of a third world nation. It had a small wealthy class, a huge class that lived in dire poverty and almost no middle class. The promise of postwar America was that the free market system would generate so much prosperity that it would pull the lower economic classes up with it, or that the wealth of the rich would "trickle down." But this is not what happened. Instead the U.S. economic class structure is looking more and more like that of the third world.

Since the Reagan years, there has been an acceleration of trends that were already underway to funnel more of America's resources into the hands of the richest part of the population. Today with international trade agreements, the small rich sectors are becoming increasingly free to make use of cheap labor in poor countries. In the U.S., the middle class is vanishing, jobs are going overseas, and a class structure similar to that of Third World countries is solidifying.

(Chomsky elaborates on this important subject in the interview immediately following this chapter.)

"What you have now is hopelessness. It's striking that about 75 percent of the population...

...thinks that the future is going to be worse than the past, that their children won't live as well as they will.

That's the first time in the history of industrial society that this has happened...

...except for during temporary things like a war.

There's a sense of permanent decline.

That's part of the reason you have all these antisocial behaviors."

[Chomsky Interview, Spin, Aug. '93]

Chomsky on Fighting Back

What can one person do?

In answer to that question, one statement of Noam Chomsky's cuts through a world of complexities and helps counteract the feeling of powerlessness that falls upon people trying to do the right thing in a complex and dangerous world:

"YOU ARE RESPONSIBLE FOR THE PREDICTABLE CONSEQUENCES OF YOUR ACTIONS."

If you do not fight back, the "predictable consequences of your actions" are more of the same: The rich get richer, the poor get poorer and more numerous. The rich and powerful, as if they were acting on orders from God, kill democracy and people in Third World countries and install dictators with whom American Interests can Do Business, using weapons and armies paid for by you to rob, torture, and kill innocent people ... and they will use the media to

TSK
TSK

blame the victims, therefore, we blame the victims, even when the victims are our own ancestors or the extended families of our lovers and friends.

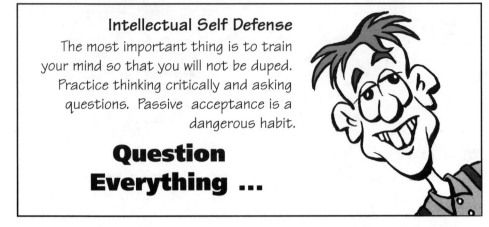

Intellectual Self Defense

The most important thing is to train your mind so that you will not be duped. Practice thinking critically and asking questions. Passive acceptance is a dangerous habit.

Question Everything ...

Every day offers opportunities to exercise your critical faculties and pay attention to what is really being said and what is really happening. You are constantly confronted with media images. If you pay attention

to what you are hearing and keep in mind who is paying the bills

to have it "brought to you by..." you can read between the lines.

Ultimately your survival may depend on how well you read what it is you are seeing. Human beings are endowed with awesome capacities for perceiving and understanding their environment, and those capacities are never more powerful than when they are engaged in survival. When you realize that your survival may be at stake, your energies focus.

The soundbite thought pattern constantly bombarding you reinforces fragmented thinking and disrupts attempts to pursue a train of thought to any sort of conclusion, or explore anything beyond its surface. But it does not prevent you from thinking about things in depth yourself, if you want to. You cannot assume that you are being told the truth or that those in charge have your best interests at heart. Such an assumption in today's world is extremely naive.

If you listen carefully and exercise your critical faculties, you can greatly enhance your chances of survival. Or you can choose to just play the game so that you stay in good with the power brokers. But who knows when it's your turn to become part of the forgotten and abandoned ones?

Interview

with
Noam Chomsky

September 14, 1993

[Cogswell] Q: What would your thoughts be about how to make your ideas accessible to a broad cross section of the public?

[Chomsky] A: There's a close interaction -- there always has been -- between what is roughly called education or discussion or discourse on the one hand, and organization on the other. They stimulate each other.

The main problem of reaching people is that almost by definition, people who are critical of established institutions and what they do will not have resources and will not have access through the established institutions except very marginally. They [the institutions] are not suicidal after all. Since that's the case, you have to establish alternative institutions, and that means organizations. Take, say, that film. [Manufacturing Consent: Noam Chomsky and the Media by Mark Achbar and Peter Wintonick], I didn't see it, but I presume it was filming talks, and those talks were possible because there are popular organizations. There's a whole complex proliferation of groups around the country and around the world in fact working on all sorts of topics and bringing people together on them, and they both have a need for speakers and they provide an opportunity for them. And then these occasions, if properly done, stimulate more interest and broader audiences. Small newspapers grow up. Community-supported radio develops. Out of the activities and the organization come opportunities for interaction among people, including talks and writing and so on, and that stimulates more of it. That's the way every movement in history ever developed, whether it was the background for the American Revolution, abolitionism, the Civil Rights movement, you pick it, that's the way it developed.

Q: Did you say you haven't seen the movie, Manufacturing Consent?

A: No actually. I've looked at the transcript, but I haven't seen the film.

Q: Unfortunately it doesn't make it into the tenplexes.

A: Well, outside of the United States it's being shown quite a lot I do a lot of traveling, I happened last year to do quite a bit of foreign traveling -- and in many countries I went to, people told me they'd seen it on national television.

The point is if people are reached individually and in an isolated fashion, it really doesn't amount to a lot. There are a lot of interesting things about American society, even unusual things. On the one hand it's a very free society, so there's very little government control, in fact by comparative standards remarkably little. On the other hand it's a very isolated society. People are really alone to an unusual extent. That's a technique of control. I mean if you're sitting alone in front of the tube, it doesn't matter a whole lot what you think.

Q: You have said that there has been a great deal of progress since the 1960s in the knowledge that people have about the nature of our governing institutions and the darker elements of our history, for example: the mass slaughter of the Native Americans. Do you think that kind of public awareness is still progressing?

A: I don't think it is at the moment. I think in a very short term focus, the last year or two, things look pretty depressing in my opinion. But over the longer term, say 30 years, I think they're encouraging. There are ups and downs.

Q: What do you see as the significance of the last election? Is there, in your view, a significant difference between a Clinton administration and a Bush administration?

A: I don't think so. I think the last election was a vote against. Clinton was one of the most unpopular candidates in recent American history. Clinton's vote, not only the percentage, but even the socioeconomic distribution of voters was very similar to Hubert Humphrey in 1968 it turns out. There was no reason for any illusions, he was quite honest about it. He put himself forward as a conservative. He was going to be what they called a New Democrat, some one who was not going to be caught up in the liberal delusions about entitlements and rights and welfare and social issues and so on, but he was going to be a business candidate, a candidate of the business community. He was pretty straightforward about that.

Q: It might be said that he was an example of what you had called "feigned dissent" because he represented a supposed alternative, but within the narrowly drawn playing field in which it is guaranteed that nothing will threaten the real powers that run the country.

A: You can't accuse him of dishonesty, he presented himself as a business-oriented conservative and that's what he is. And I think that the reason for the lack of popular support, which was quite low, was because.... I mean you know a lot of people didn't like Bush, so there was a lot of negative vote. But I think people are looking for anything.

In this respect the Perot candidacy was kind of interesting. When Perot appeared on the scene -- it was spring '92 I think -- he had no platform at all. He just said, "Look at me! I'm a rich guy with big ears -

- vote for me!" And within a week or two he was running even with the major candidates. I think they would have voted for Mickey Mouse. Even those who voted for Clinton were not very enthusiastic according to public opinion studies.

Q: What do you think of Gore -- his backing by military groups and his stated support of environmental protection?

A: Gore is another neo-liberal, much beloved by people around the New Republic for example. I mean he has some words to say, I don't know if there's anything behind the words about the environment but that's about it. The Clinton military budget is a natural extension of the Bush one. It hasn't changed a lot.

Q: How does the Clinton foreign policy compare to the Bush one?

A: About the same. I mean there are changes taking place, but that's because of changes in the world and changes in the economy. The domestic population is much less willing to support military intervention than it was in the past. The Bush administration was well aware of that.

Q: What effect do you think the Gulf War had on the election?

A: Well, you know the Gulf War aroused a wave of jingoism and also extraordinary fear. This is a very frightened country. It was quite interesting. I traveled around a lot during that period and I went, in fact, to the most jingoist and reactionary parts of the country where I could get an invitation and it was remarkable to see how frightened people were. But this is a very frightened country. It's been noticed for a long time in Europe. Every couple of years the tourist industry in Europe collapses because Americans are afraid to go to European cities where they are about 100 times as safe as in any American city and there's a lot of joking and laughter about it there, and ridicule.

But you could see it during the Gulf War, people were really scared that Saddam was going to come and get 'em. But after the war, actually it's hard to work out, but a number of economists think the war was probably profitable for the United States, that is, the amount of money that was ripped off of Germany and Japan and the Gulf States probably more than paid for the U.S. costs. But I think what was tricky was that the aftermath of the Gulf War was pretty hard to deal with, if you looked at what was left. There was a tremendous amount of devasta-

tion. The Gulf monarchies or dictatorships were firmly in power, not a move towards democratization or anything else. Saddam Hussein was back in power firmly. He was slaughtering his own population and the U.S. was standing back and applauding silently. There's a human rights disaster developing in Iraq primarily after the war. Probably 100,000 children or so have died after the war from the sanctions and so on. That's not a pretty picture and it had to be suppressed pretty quickly. That's one of the reasons why they took off all at once into this fanfare about a Middle East peace process, to try turn people's attention away from it. The Gulf War left a bad taste. For one thing people could see that the fear and hysteria were manufactured. They had to be able to understand after this that we were fighting a defenseless third world country. It was pretty hard to suppress that after February.

Q: You have written and spoken about Carter's move to send arms to Indonesia to help the Indonesian government slaughter the natives of East Timor. This certainly runs counter to the prevailing image of Carter as a decent, peace-seeking man. Was he just a hypocrite? Was this something that happened without his full

awareness of the consequences of what he was doing? Was it tacked onto other legislation?

A: This was a Carter initiative. Not only did they radically increase the flow of aid to Indonesia, but Walter Mondale, who was then vice president, flew to Jakarta in 1978. That was the period of the worst atrocities -- which were well known incidentally, I mean the press wasn't reporting them, but there were plenty of other sources. Surely U.S. intelligence knew all about it. Mondale went to Jakarta. He was terribly impressed by how wonderful it was. He telegraphed back to Washington that they ought to send them more jet planes. Carter couldn't do that because of congressional legislation that prevented direct military aid to human rights violators, so they arranged with Israel to ship American jets to Indonesia. That was all White House initiatives.

Q: What could have been his motivations?

A: His motivations were "stability" and the usual things. When you ask whether Carter was a hypocrite or not, I haven't the slightest idea. You'd have to get into his head and find out. Maybe he believed he was doing the right thing, who knows? In my opinion, these are not very interesting questions. Most people, we all know from our own personal experiences, if not from reading history, that it's very easy to construct a pattern of justifiction for just about anything you choose to do. I mean none of us are so saintly that we haven't done ugly and unpleasant things in our lives, like maybe you took a toy from your five-year-old brother when you were a kid or something. Just ask yourself, anybody can ask themselves, how often did I say to myself, "Boy I'm really rotten, but this is what I feel like doing." Very rarely. Usually you set up a pattern of justification that makes it exactly the right thing to do. That's the way beliefs are formed.

Motivations are kind of hidden. If you're honest, maybe you could dig out and find them, but it's awfully easy and a common experience to construct a pattern of justification for things you do out of some kind of self interest. And that's done in statecraft all the time. So the question whether someone's being hypocritical or not is almost meaningless.

His motivations are straightforward. Indonesia's a very rich country, huge resources which were open to exploitation by foreign corporations. Suharto, the head, was keeping the country under control.

If you want to know the motivation, I suggest if you're interested you might have a look at, I have a book that came out about a year ago called *Year 501* and one of the chapters in it reviews the western reaction to the military coup that brought Suharto to office in 1965. He immediately launched the biggest slaughter since the holocaust. Nobody knows how many, but maybe seven- or eight-hundred thousand people were slaughtered in four months. Huge bloodbath, *Time* magazine called it "a boiling bloodbath." Most of the people killed were landless peasants. It destroyed the only popular organization in the country, namely the Indonesian Communist Party, mostly the peasant party. What's interesting about it was the reaction of the west, which was total euphoria. The New York Times described it as "a gleam of light in Asia." News magazines were writing about "hope where there once was none." New York Times editorials, which I run through closely in this, thought it was just magnificent. The more the boiling bloodbath boiled the more they loved it. It wasn't even hidden. It was quite open. It was a very interesting episode. It's a lot of detail about it there and the point was very straightforward: this vindicated the US war in Vietnam. In fact American liberals were writing that

this proves that we were right to be in Vietnam because in Vietnam we were providing a shield which encouraged the Indonesian generals to get on with the necessary work of cleansing their own society and throwing it open to western robbers. It was remarkably open. Take a look at the quotes. I went through a very comprehensive review then -- complete euphoria. A lot of the reason why the Vietnam war was fought was to protect the surrounding regions from the infection of popular uprisings. The most brutal dictatorship we supported was in Indonesia, but at the same time we also supported very bloody dictatorships and coups in other surrounding countries in Thailand, the Marcos coup in the Philippines and so on, all for the same reasons. So sure, that's the motivation.

Q: In what ways do you perceive that our progress is slowed in terms of the general awareness of these things at the moment?

A: For one thing there's an incredible degree of conformism setting in even more than usual. To a remarkable extent people say the same thing and think the same thoughts. You hear the same fabrications and so on, with less and less in the way of critical voices. And as far as the popular movements are concerned, I think that they're dissipating a lot of energy on inside issues, many of them. There's a lot of self-destruction in my opinion.

Take for example all this frenzy about the JFK assassination. I mean I don't know who assassinated him and I don't care, but what difference does it make? It's not an issue of any general political interest. And there's a huge amount of energy and effort going into that.

If somebody could show that there was some general significance to the assassination, that it changed policy, or that there was some high-level involvement or whatever, then it would be an important historical event. Other than that, it's just like the killing of anyone else. Naturally you're somebody gets killed, but why is it an issue for the popular movements anymore than the latest killing on the streets of Hoboken?

The Left -- I use the term loosely -- the whole array of popular movements and dissident groups and so on have spent huge energy and effort in this. That's one example. There are others.

Q: Your book *Rethinking Camelot* makes a powerful case against the theory that JFK was removed because he was intending to pull out of Vietnam.

A: Really the book is not about the Kennedy assassination. What it's about is the buildup to the war in Vietnam, which we now know a lot about because of recent documentation, and it shows very clearly what was going on. Kennedy just launched an attack against South Vietnam and hadn't the slightest intent of ending it short of victory. Also interesting, at least I thought it was interesting, in the last chapter I went through the accounts that have been given of that period, and it's very striking to see. There were a lot of memoirs written at the time by people like Arthur Schlesinger and others, and all of these memoirists completely revised their account after the Tet Offensive in January of 1968 that made the war unpopular. American corporate elites decided at that point that it just wasn't worth it, it was too costly, let's pull out. So at that time everybody became an opponent of the war because the orders from on high were that you were supposed to be opposed to it. And after that every single memoirist radically changed their story about what had happened. They all concocted this story that their hero, John F. Kennedy, was really planning to pull out of this unpopular war before he was killed and then Johnson changed it. If you look at the earlier memoirs, not a hint, I mean literally. Like Schlesinger in his 940 page book has less about the withdrawal than the New York Times did. And it's not that any new information came along, it didn't. The new information that came along just showed more that he had no intention of withdrawing. But the war became unpopular, therefore people had to rewrite the story. And they did it in the most amazing way. I mean this is the kind of thing you might have found in Stalinist Russia and it happened right here in a free country.

Q: What kinds of political activities are meaningful? What can people do that would really make a difference?

A: There are things. I mean I don't think there are any real formulas. Some participation in electoral politics is sometimes very important. I personally myself almost always vote at least in local elections where things often make a difference. National politics, in my opinion, often doesn't make much of a difference. There are groups, take say the New Party, the political organization. I mean I think they have a pretty sane program. They're looking forward to trying to ultimately be a force in electoral politics. Their shorter term concern is to influence local politics and sup-

port a lot more progressive candidates elsewhere and to use their electoral participation as an organization technique. I mean, after all, a lot of attention is focused on elections -- whether they're meaningful or not is sort of beside the point in this respect -- and that attention can be used to bring up issues to create more lasting organizations that bring people together to work systematically right after the election. The important thing is to keep the work up after the election. If elections are just something where you go in, then you push a button and then you go home, then it doesn't make much difference which button you push.

Q: Do you feel positive about the future?

A: Whether a person feels positive or not is kind of a comment on their personality and of no great interest. You can find positive signs or you can find negative signs. How you evaluate them depends on what happened in your life recently or something like that. There's no objective way to do it. The important thing is to try to commit yourself to making the positive signs more real. Suppose that you felt that there's 99 percent of a probability that human civilization is going to be destroyed in the next hundred years, but one percent chance that it won't be, and that one percent offers some opportunities to do something. Well you commit yourself to that one percent.

Q: How do you get from discussion groups to, say, anarcho-syndicalism?

A: Just a more democratic society, let's not give it any fancy words. A world that's under the thumb of huge transnational corporations and the institutions that cater to them, that is not a democratic world, even if you have elections.

Q: Do you see the new technologies, by helping to increase the flow of information, to be a force toward decentralization of power or toward more democracy?

A: Certainly not in the rich countries. Take, say, the United States -- which is not unusual; we're like other rich countries -- the United States developed its own economy behind very high protectionist walls, with enormous state intervention and it maintains it that way. The Pentagon system, for example, is itself a huge government program arranged for a taxpayer subsidy to advanced industry. I can't imagine anything more

radically opposed to the free market. In fact even the things that are called free trade agreements, like say NAFTA, are not free trade agreements. For one thing, they

don't deal particularly with trade, and for another, they're not free. NAFTA has enormous protectionist elements built into it which is one of the main reasons why a lot of American industry supports it .

Very important things are happening in the United States and other countries. It's not a big secret that the economy is moving very fast, in fact, from what used to be mainly national economies to an increasingly internationalized economy. So take say the United States: 30 years ago the question of international trade was not a big issue because the national economy was so huge in comparison with trade that it didn't matter all that much. You didn't have big debates about trade policy. Now that's changed. The international economy is enormous. In fact it's not really trade, so about 40 percent of U.S. trade, as it's called, is actually internal to big transnational corporations. It means like one branch of the Ford Motor Company moving things to another branch which happens to be across a border. Forty percent is not a small amount, and it's the same world-wide. But, in any event, the economy's becoming much more internationalized. It's much easier to move capital abroad. The effect of that is that production can be shifted much more easily to low-wage/high-repression areas elsewhere. And the effect of that is to bring the third world model home to the United States and other rich countries. It means that these countries themselves are drifting toward a kind of a third world model in which there's a sector of great wealth and privilege and a growing mass of people who are basically superfluous. They're not necessary for a profit either as producers or consumers. You can produce more cheaply elsewhere and the market can easily become the international wealthy sectors. You end up with south-central Los Angeles and that's happening more and more. That's going to create very big changes and what's more that's going to continue as long as decisions over investment are in private hands. It's not a law of nature: the private enterprise system, which is of course a state-subsidized, publicly subsidized private enterprise system, that is deeply anti-democratic by its very nature. It means that the basic decisions of human life are out of the framework of popular influence and control, and that's not a law of nature.

Q: Thomas Jefferson, as author of the Declaration of Independence, is certainly a symbol of the spirit of American democracy, a hero even to those who feel that later political leaders lost track of the ideals of the founding fathers, but in your book you show documents of Jefferson sending out soldiers with orders to wipe out entire villages of the Cherokees. Is there no one that can be used as a positive example?

A: We shouldn't be looking for heroes, we should be looking for good ideas. They are mixed. Jefferson's attitudes towards democracy were generally good, his attitudes towards freedom of religion were quite good. His attitude toward freedom of speech, on the other hand, was not good at all. Let alone extermination of the native population. These are human beings after all, like each of us is. If we look into ourselves honestly, we'll find an odd mixture. ■

Index

HOW TO GET GREAT THINKERS
TO COME TO OUR HOME...

To order any current titles of Writers and Readers **For Beginners**™ books, please fill out the coupon below and enclose a check made out to **Writers and Readers Publishing, Inc.** To order by phone (with Master Card or Visa), or to receive a <u>free catalog</u> of all our **For Beginners**™ books, please call (212) 982-3158.

Individual Order Form   (clip out or copy complete page)

Book Title	Quantity	Amount
	Sub Total:	
N.Y. residents add 8 1/4% sales tax		
Shipping & Handling ($3.00 for the first book; $.60 for each additional book)		
	TOTAL	

Name _____

Address _____

City _____ State _____ Zip Code _____

Phone number (___) _____

MC / VISA (circle one)   Account # _____ Expires _____

Addiction & Recovery ($11.00)
African History ($9.95)
Arabs & Israel ($11.00)
Architecture ($11.00)
Babies ($9.95)
Biology ($11.00)
Black History ($9.95)
Black Holocaust ($11.00)
Black Panthers ($11.00)
Black Women ($9.95)
Brecht ($9.95)
Classical Music ($9.95)
Computers ($11.00)
DNA ($9.95)
Domestic Violence ($11.00)
Elvis ($6.95)
Erotica ($7.95)
Food ($7.95)
Foucault ($9.95)
Freud ($9.95)
Health Care ($9.95)
Heidegger ($9.95)
Hemingway ($9.95)
History of Clowns ($11.00)
Ireland ($9.95)
Islam ($9.95)
Jazz ($11.00)
Jewish Holocaust ($11.00)
J.F.K. ($9.95)
Judaism ($9.95)
Kierkegaard ($11.00)
Malcolm X ($9.95)
Mao ($9.95)
Martial Arts ($11.00)
Miles Davis ($9.00)
Nietzsche ($9.95)
Opera ($11.00)
Orwell ($4.95)
Pan-Africanism ($9.95)
Philosophy ($11.00)
Plato ($11.00)
Psychiatry ($9.95)
Rainforests ($7.95)
Sartre ($11.00)
Saussure ($11.00)
Sex ($9.95)
UNICEF ($11.00)
United Nations ($11.00)
World War II ($8.95)
Zen ($11.00)

Send check or money order to: **Writers and Readers Publishing**, P.O. Box 461 Village Station, New York, NY 10014 1-(800) 860-2139; (212) 982-3158, fx (212) 777-4924; In the U.K: **Airlift Book Company**, 8, The Arena, Mollison Ave., Enfield, EN3 7NJ, England 0181.804.0044. Or contact us for a <u>FREE</u> <u>CATALOG</u> of all our For Beginners™ titles.

Writers and Readers